THE BOOK OF

TOTALLY
IRRESPONSIBLE
SCIENCE

THE BOOK OF
# TOTALLY
# IRRESPONSIBLE
# SCIENCE

## SEAN CONNOLLY

WORKMAN PUBLISHING
NEW YORK

Library of Congress Cataloging-in-Publication Data is available.

ISBN 978-0-7611-5020-6

Workman books are available at special discounts when purchased
in bulk for premiums and sales promotions as well as for fund-
raising or educational use. Special editions or book excerpts can
also be created to specification. For details, contact the
Special Sales Director at the address below.

Mentos® is a registered trademark of
Perfetti Van Melle Benelux B.V Corporation

Cover illustrations by Lou Brooks

Design by Robb Allen and Netta Rabin
Chapter opener art written and illustrated by Lou Brooks
Method illustrations by Robert James

Workman Publishing Company, Inc.
225 Varick Street
New York, NY 10014-4381
www.workman.com

Printed in the United States of America

First printing September 2008
10 9 8 7 6 5 4

*To my companions on this wonderful journey—*
*Frederika, Jamie, Anna, Thomas, and Dafydd*

# CONTENTS

## Chapter One

# CORE CONCERNS

## Chapter Two

# HARNESSING THE ELEMENTS

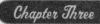

# Chapter Three

# FOOD FOR THOUGHT

# Chapter Four

# HOW MOVING!

# A LOT OF HOT AIR

# 100% NATURAL

# MAD SCIENCE

# LAST WORDS

# AT A GLANCE

# TOTALLY IRRESPONSIBLE NOTES

take me to
YOUR ReaDeR . . .

# INTRODUCTION

*The Oxford Dictionary of English* defines science as "the intellectual and practical activity encompassing the systematic study of the structure and behavior of the physical and natural world through observation and experiment."

This definition explains the link between humankind's earliest paintings—with their vivid depictions of cave lions and predatory wolves—and the NASA space shuttle studies of atmospheric winds using laser radar. Through the ages, whether or not they called themselves "scientists," people have observed and experimented their way to a better understanding of the world and how it works.

Throughout our history, we have been driven by curiosity and the "need to know." Scientists have probed all manner of conundrums, teasing out answers and sharing their findings. Just think of how much of our knowledge can be traced to questions such as:

Why does the sun rise and set every day?

Why did that ripe apple fall down from the tree and not up?

If water expands when it becomes steam, could it be used to drive a piston?

Could more than one computer be linked together using, say, a telephone connection?

We know—or know how to find out—the answers to these and thousands of other questions that have inspired scientists through the ages. And we can see the benefits all around us, especially in the field of technology, which harnesses the advances of science and turns them to practical advantage.

## NEW SETS OF QUESTIONS

*The Book of Totally Irresponsible Science* carries on this noble tradition of scientific exploration and takes it to new—yet, in many ways, familiar—areas. After all, the quest for knowledge does not end when we hang up our goggles and turn off the light in the science lab. The everyday world provides us with the tools to carry on with our scientific probing.

The 64 experiments described in the following pages use ingredients or materials found in most households or which can be easily bought. Like the classic scientific experiments, which use questions as launching pads for inquiry, these experiments also seek to find and demonstrate answers. Some of the answers, however, might well tie in with a completely different set of questions—along the lines of:

"What's that straw doing inside a potato?"

"Son, have you seen my blow-dryer?"

"What in the world has happened to this geranium?"

"Wait a minute! Is that my new Black Eyed Peas CD floating around over there?"

## THE "I" WORD

All of this brings us to an important word in the title of this book: *irresponsible*. Where does being irresponsible tie in with conducting experiments? Isn't it the opposite of the scientific method? Or is it possible that there could be more than one reading of the word *irresponsible*?

Kids, for instance, are always being labeled "irresponsible": by their parents because they don't clean their rooms, or walk their dogs, or keep their schoolwork neat and tidy. But for kids, these "responsible" duties simply get in the way of their "irresponsible" pursuits, like climbing trees or building sand castles. These activities, which are fueled by their curiosity and imagination, can be considered "irresponsible" to a certain degree, but it is exactly this definition of the "i" word that I wish to employ in this book. By that definition, each of the experiments certainly does merit the descriptive term "irresponsible."

Although using the "i" word, *The Book of Totally Irresponsible Science* advocates due care and attention in each experiment. The presentation of each experiment is straightforward and logical, right down to any words of special warning that apply to the experiment. So please do take care when doing all these experiments.

## WHO CAN DO THESE EXPERIMENTS?

*The Book of Totally Irresponsible Science* offers everyone, young or old, the chance to enter the fascinating world of science. For kids, who may just be entering this world, this book offers the opportunity to witness firsthand the almost magical appeal of basic physics and chemistry. But while we hope for the active participation of budding young scientists whenever possible, these experiments should always be conducted under adult supervision. Bear in mind that the responsibility for each experiment lies with the adult supervising it. These experiments are *for* children as well as adults, but they are not to be conducted *by* children without adults.

The final section of each experiment, **Take Care!**, highlights any particular warnings relevant to the experiment. Some of these are no more than bits of friendly advice on how to get the best effects. Others have a more practical aim of drawing the reader's attention to ingredients or actions that call for extra care. A special **Match Alert!** is a prominent flag to any experiment that involves matches or an open flame.

Apart from producing a result that will amuse, enchant, or possibly even inspire, each experiment is presented in a form that most of us recognize: a simple recipe.

## HOW THIS BOOK WORKS

The 64 entries in *The Book of Totally Irresponsible Science* are grouped into seven chapters, each representing a different scientific theme or intended result.

A typical entry introduces the nature of the experiment and what to expect, before breaking it down into the following sections:

**Time Factor:** The time—from the first stage of preparation to the *oohs* and *aahs* at the conclusion—that it will take to perform this experiment. You might have a whole weekend free or only a few minutes to spare, so each experiment will have this handy guideline. You will also find a list in the back of this book grouping the experiments in order of time required.

**You Will Need:** A straightforward list of ingredients.

**Take Care!** Special advice (and in some cases, warnings) for the experiment.

**Method:** Numbered step-by-step and easy-to-follow instructions.

**The Scientific Excuse:** The raison d'être for the experiment, or possibly your hurried explanation to an impatient or angry parent!

## FINAL WORDS

So, isn't it time you went out and built that volcano you've always wanted to build? Or maybe you want to make your own ice cream in a coffee can? Perhaps you've decided you're ready to change the color scheme in your living room, *starting with the plants that are already there*! The following pages will let you do all of these things and much more, all in a spirit of playful scientific inquiry.

For most of the experiments, a broad smile and an open mind will count for far more than a white coat and a calculator. So throw yourself into these funny, eye-opening, quirky experiments and see where they take you. And in the process you'll have a chance to learn—and maybe even teach others—a little science!

# · The · EXPERIMENTS

# Chapter One

# CORE CONCERNS

A t times the Earth seems like a child trying to wriggle out of a coat that's just too small. Chasms open, the ground shakes with quakes and tremors, while magma, lava, hot water, and steam burst through the planet's crust with dramatic effect. The experiments in this chapter offer a glimpse of the basic physics that lie behind these "earth-shattering" events. Cooking ingredients, basic kitchen equipment, and even candy all play their part in explaining some of these basic forces.

# Cola GEYSER

*chill, dude*

**SOME OF THE MOST MEMORABLE EXPERIMENTS CAN BE DONE** with ingredients that don't seem in the least "scientific." For example, you can mix a popular candy and an even more popular soft drink to create your own version of Old Faithful. The volatile mixture sends a geyser as high as 20 feet.

## You Will Need

- **PACKAGE OF MENTOS CANDIES**
- **TEST TUBE**
- **2-INCH-SQUARE PIECE OF CARDBOARD**
- **2-LITER PLASTIC BOTTLE OF DIET COLA**

*TAKE CARE!* **DO THIS EXPERIMENT OUTDOORS, WELL AWAY FROM ANYTHING (OR ANYONE) YOU WOULDN'T WANT TO BECOME A STICKY WET MESS. UNLESS YOU WANT SOMETHING—OR SOMEONE—TO BECOME A STICKY WET MESS, IN WHICH CASE YOU SHOULD PERFORM THIS EXPERIMENT AT YOUR OWN RISK!**

# METHOD

**1** Put 12 Mentos candies in a test tube and hold the cardboard to the open top of the tube.

**2** Open the bottle of diet cola and put the test tube upside down on top of the open bottle, still holding the cardboard in place.

**3** Take care to know which way to run.

**4** Slide the cardboard away quickly so that the candies drop in.

**5** Run clear and watch as the cola explodes out of the bottle.

## The Scientific Excuse

This explosive reaction comes from the sudden release of carbon dioxide, the gas that gives soda its bubbles. This carbon dioxide normally remains dissolved in the soda because there are no nucleation sites—irregularities around which bubbles can form. Seen close up, a single Mento has a craggy surface—providing hundreds of nucleation sites. A dozen of those candies dumped in at once sets off a massive release of carbon dioxide, forcing the cola out of the bottle like a rocket. Diet cola works best because most non-diet colas use corn syrup, which suppresses the formation of bubbles.

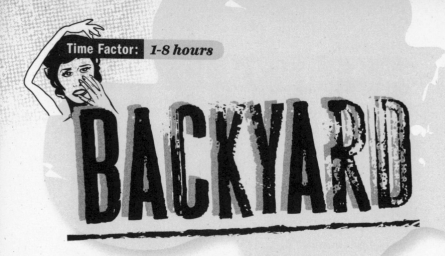

# BACKYARD

THIS VIVID DISPLAY OF A CHEMICAL REACTION ISN'T dangerous, but it earns its place in this book by being very, very messy. It goes without saying that this is an outdoor experiment, so make sure you choose a dry (low humidity) day to demonstrate those dramatic lava flows. And if you're feeling really resourceful, you can add some to-scale model houses at the base of the volcano.

## *You Will Need*

- 3-FEET-SQUARE PLYWOOD SHEET
- EMPTY 1-LITER BOTTLE (GLASS OR PLASTIC)
- MODELING CLAY OR PAPIER-MÂCHÉ (ENOUGH TO FORM A "VOLCANIC CONE" ABOUT 13 INCHES ACROSS AT ITS BASE)
- 1 TABLESPOON BAKING SODA
- 2 TEASPOONS DISHWASHING LIQUID
- RED OR YELLOW FOOD COLORING
- 1/4 CUP VINEGAR

# VESUVIUS

# METHOD

**1** Put the empty bottle in the middle of the plywood sheet. It will be the center of the volcano.

**2** Build the volcano around this bottle, using either modeling clay or papier-mâché.

**3** Work on and decorate the volcano while it is still soft, carving out gulleys and ravines for the lava flows.

*TAKE CARE!* THE BIGGEST PROBLEM WITH THIS EXPERIMENT IS THE POSSIBLE MESS, BUT GIVING TOO MUCH OF A WARNING HERE WOULD BE OVERDOING IT, WOULDN'T IT? BESIDES, WHAT'S A VOLCANO WITHOUT A LITTLE MESS?

**4** Make sure the finished volcano has enough time to dry.

**5** Add the baking soda, dishwashing liquid, and a squirt of food coloring to the empty bottle.

**6** Measure out the vinegar and pour it into the bottle.

Boom!

**7** Stand back as the forces of nature take over!

## The Scientific Excuse

The trigger for the eruption is the addition of the vinegar (an acid) to the earlier mixture, which is basic (the opposite of acidic) thanks to the inclusion of baking soda. Adding the vinegar triggers an "acid/base neutralization," as chemists would put it. More specifically, this reaction changes carbonic acid into water and carbon dioxide; the liberated carbon dioxide leads to the dramatic foaming.

# The Sandwich-
# BAG BOMB

K IDS—AND MANY GROWN-UPS—MAY THINK of acids and bases as harmful chemicals that white-coated scientists keep locked away. This experiment is a simple way of showing that a kitchen cupboard has these chemical "secret agents" in abundance. And with just a little outlay in time and equipment, you can get "more bang for your buck," as the saying goes.

## You Will Need

- A ZIPLOCK SANDWICH BAG
- PAPER TOWEL
- 1 1/2 TABLESPOONS BAKING SODA
- 1/2 CUP VINEGAR
- 1/4 CUP WARM WATER

**TAKE CARE!** NO ONE IS GOING TO GET HURT IN THIS EXPERIMENT, BUT IT CAN PRODUCE A MESS. CHOOSE YOUR SPOT CAREFULLY BEFOREHAND, MAKING SURE NOTHING—AND NOBODY—WILL GET SOAKED OR SOILED—UNLESS, OF COURSE, YOU WANT TO "SURPRISE" SOMEBODY WHO ENJOYS A GOOD LOUD POP EVERY NOW AND AGAIN!

# METHOD

**1** This experiment will work only if your sandwich bag has no holes. Test it by half-filling it with water, zipping it shut, and turning it upside down over the sink.

**2** If no water leaks out, you're fine. Empty out the test water.

**3** Tear a sheet of paper towel into a square measuring about 6 inches x 6 inches.

**4** Pour the baking soda onto the center of the paper towel, then fold the towel into an "envelope" with the powder inside it.

**5** Pour the vinegar and warm water into the bag.

**6** Then, carefully but quickly, add the paper towel "envelope" to the bag and seal it.

**7** Shake the bag a little, then put it on the ground and stand back.

**8** The bag will inflate and then pop with a satisfying bang.

**BOOM!**

### The Scientific Excuse

The vinegar and baking soda react dramatically and quickly, producing carbon dioxide in equal portions as a result. This carbon dioxide soon fills the bag and then, after straining at the bag's seams, pops it with a bang.

# *Flameproof*
# BALLOON

HERE IS ANOTHER ONE OF THOSE "LESS IS MORE" EXPERI-ments. With precious little investment (how much does a balloon cost, after all?) and no real preparation, you can perform an experiment that is a real eye-opener. Balloons are always popping, aren't they? Yet why won't this one burst when it's placed in an open flame?

**MATCH ALERT!**
This experiment involves the use of matches and should be conducted only with a responsible adult present.

## You Will Need

- BALLOON (STRONG ENOUGH TO HOLD WATER)
- TAP WATER; OR A 2-LITER BOTTLE FULL OF WATER (OPTIONAL)
- MATCHES
- CANDLE

*TAKE CARE!* **BLOW OUT THE CANDLE AFTER PERFORMING THE EXPERIMENT.**

# METHOD

**1** Fill the balloon with water until it is about the size of a grapefruit. You can do this by fitting the mouth of the balloon over a faucet and filling it with cold water. Alternatively, if you're away from a water tap, fit the balloon over the mouth of a bottle of water.

**2** Tie the mouth of the balloon in a secure knot and shake it so that any excess drops of water fall off.

**3** Light the candle and place it somewhere secure.

**4** Hold the balloon by pinching the knotted end and move it into the flame.

**5** Keep the balloon in the flame for a few seconds, then remove it.

**6** Repeat the process—the balloon seems to be flameproof!

## The Scientific Excuse

This experiment tells us a lot about heat absorption. If you held a balloon filled with air in the flame, it would burst quickly. The heat of the flame would weaken the rubber until it could no longer withstand the pressure of the air inside. Water, however, absorbs heat very well. This means that the water inside the balloon absorbs the heat of the flame, leaving the rubber more or less unscathed.

# BEACON FROM

**THE ADVANCED CIVILIZATION OF ATLANTIS VANISHED** beneath the waves before the time of the ancient Greeks. With it went—so the story goes—a wealth of knowledge never to be recovered. But maybe not all of these skills have disappeared. How else could you explain a candle staying lit even when it's under water? It must be a message from below.

# ATLANTIS

## *You Will Need*

- 1½-INCH DIAMETER VOTIVE CANDLE (AS TALL AS THE BOWL IS HIGH)
- BREAKFAST CEREAL BOWL (PREFERABLY CLEAR)
- WATER
- MATCHES

## METHOD

**1** Place the candle in the center of the bowl, pointing upward.

**2** Carefully fill the bowl with water right up to the top of the candle.

**3** Light the candle and observe.

**4** In time, the candlewick will burn down, even below the water level, and melt a wax funnel around itself.

**5** The flame, protected by the funnel, will continue to burn for some time below water level.

way down below the ocean, where I wanna be...

## The Scientific Excuse

Normally, in the open air, the wax by the wick would melt and either evaporate or flow down the side of the candle. But water is excellent at absorbing heat, and *it* draws the warmth that would otherwise melt the wax. So instead of melting, the wax remains in its solid funnel shape, guarding the flame like a dike against the water outside.

# CAN YOU HOLD, PLEASE?

THERE'S A LITTLE BIT OF MAGIC IN EVERY SCIENTIFIC experiment, whether it concentrates on the tiniest particles or the speed of light through the infinity of space. This experiment inhabits that land of wonder and mystery, beginning as a puzzle and usually ending up with applause and laughter. Maybe it's best if you frame it as a challenge to an adult with some money to spare: "How much do you want to bet that I can pick up this ice cube from the pie plate without getting my fingers wet?" The level of irresponsibility inherent in this particular experiment is directly proportional to the amount of money you're willing to take!

## You Will Need

- ICE CUBE
- ALUMINUM-FOIL PIE PLATE
- 6 INCHES OF STRING
- TABLE SALT

*TAKE CARE!* MAKE SURE YOU LIFT THE TWO ENDS OF STRING GENTLY, SINCE A SUDDEN JERK WILL ALMOST CERTAINLY YANK THE STRING FROM THE PROTECTIVE LAYER OF ICE.

# METHOD

**1** Rinse the ice cube in water and set it down on the pie plate.

**2** Lay the string across the ice cube.

**3** Sprinkle salt on top of the ice cube, making sure much of it lands on or near the string.

**4** Wait about 15 seconds and then hold the ends of the string.

**5** Slowly lift the string, which will be holding the ice cube.

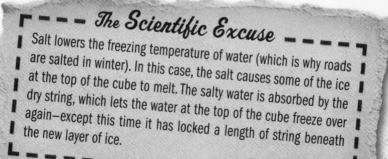

## The Scientific Excuse

Salt lowers the freezing temperature of water (which is why roads are salted in winter). In this case, the salt causes some of the ice at the top of the cube to melt. The salty water is absorbed by the dry string, which lets the water at the top of the cube freeze over again—except this time it has locked a length of string beneath the new layer of ice.

# Chapter Two

# HARNESSING the ELEMENTS

**F**reddie Mercury's words, "Thunderbolts and lightning, very very frightening," in the pop group Queen's song "Bohemian Rhapsody" hit a raw nerve. Since the dawn of history, human beings have been fascinated and frightened in equal measure by the power of the elements. And while we have a better explanation for these phenomena than, say, the ancient Greeks, we still have a hard time linking them to everyday forces around us. The following experiments call on familiar ingredients—flour, water, pie plates, and ballpoint pens—to demonstrate how weather works.

# HOMEMADE

**WHAT'S WEATHER TALK WITHOUT A LITTLE EXAGGERATION** now and then? Okay, well, maybe real lightning is a few trillion times more powerful, but this experiment goes right to the heart of the science that produces a lightning bolt—an electrical discharge. In the case of real lightning, this discharge goes from cloud to cloud. Here the distance and scale are more modest—the breadth of a fingernail. But with the lights out and a good explanation, this can be a real crowd-pleaser—especially if you enlist the help of a younger brother or sister. "Hey, Mom, do you mind if I drop a little lightning bolt on Jack? Thanks!"

# LIGHTNING

## *You Will Need*

- THUMBTACK
- ALUMINUM-FOIL PIE PLATE
- GLUE, IF NEEDED

- BALLPOINT PEN
- 12-INCH X 4-INCH X 1-INCH STYROFOAM BLOCK
- WOOL SOCK

# METHOD

 Push the thumbtack from the back of the pie plate through the center.

 Press the non-writing end of the pen into the tack point, securing with glue if needed.

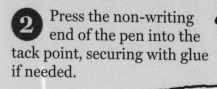

 Quickly rub the Styrofoam block with the wool sock.

**TAKE CARE!** THE FOLLOWING IS NOT A SAFETY WARNING (THIS IS ONE OF THE SAFEST EXPERIMENTS IN THE BOOK). FILE IT INSTEAD UNDER "FOLLOW THIS ADVICE IF YOU WANT THE EXPERIMENT TO WORK." MAKE SURE YOU ARE HOLDING THE PEN WHEN YOU PLACE THE PIE PLATE ON THE STYROFOAM. OTHERWISE, THE EXCESS ELECTRONS WILL FLOW UNDRAMATICALLY FROM STYROFOAM TO PIE PLATE TO FINGER.

**4** Using the pen as a handle, pick up the pie plate (not touching the plate itself).

**5** Put the pie plate down carefully on the Styrofoam.

**6** Turn out the lights. Draw your finger closer and closer to the pie plate.

**7** You should see, hear, and feel a small spark.

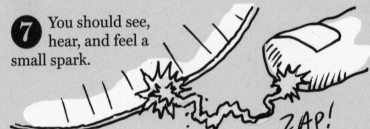

ZAP!

## The Scientific Excuse

The sock rubbing causes (negatively charged) electrons to flow from the wool to the Styrofoam, giving it a negative charge. Similar charges (positive and positive or negative and negative) repel each other, so the electrons of the Styrofoam cause some of the electrons in the pie plate to move away from the Styrofoam. The electrons are waiting to escape from the pie plate, but cannot move through the pen (because it is an insulator). They can, however, flow through the human body and jump across the small gap to reach the experimenter's finger.

# HEAVY WEATHER?

**GLOBAL WARMING, CARBON EMISSIONS, THE OZONE LAYER—** it can all seem a little baffling, especially for young people with relatively little science background. But given a chance to create some carbon dioxide—and then see how it's a force to be reckoned with—you might want to learn a little more about carbon offsetting. Plus, there's always something spooky about invisible forces at work around us. Build yourself a homemade scale to prove that the invisible carbon dioxide is heavier than the equally invisible air.

## You Will Need

- THUMBTACK
- TAPE
- 2 CLEAR PLASTIC BAGS (SANDWICH BAG SIZE)
- 12-INCH RULER
- ½ CUP VINEGAR
- 3 TEASPOONS BAKING SODA
- DRINKING GLASS

# METHOD

**1** Place the thumbtack pointing up near the corner of a table.

**2** Tape an open plastic bag (leaving a good upward-facing opening) to each end of the ruler.

**3** Carefully balance the ruler on the thumbtack point to create a homemade scale.

**4** Mix the vinegar and baking soda in the drinking glass.

**5** When this mixture begins to froth, carefully tilt the glass over one of the open plastic bags. Do not actually pour any of the liquid, or even the froth.

**6** The bag beneath the glass should slowly sink under the weight of the invisible new ingredient.

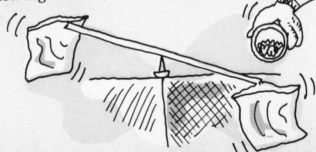

**TAKE CARE!** TILT THE GLASS GENTLY ONCE YOU HAVE MIXED THE VINEGAR AND THE BAKING SODA. HAVING GONE TO THE TROUBLE OF CREATING THE DELICATE SCALE, YOU DON'T WANT TO BLOW THE EXPERIMENT BY POURING THE LIQUID INTO THE BAG—THE WHOLE POINT IS THAT THE BAG IS DRAGGED DOWN BY THE INVISIBLE GAS!

## The Scientific Excuse

A diligent science student will recognize that mixing vinegar and baking soda is one of the best—and easiest—ways of producing carbon dioxide. Carbon dioxide is a by-product of the reaction between am acid (vinegar) and a base (baking soda). Moreover, carbon dioxide is heavier than air. That's why it can be poured, just as one could pour a liquid into one of the bags, causing the scale to tip.

# *Static Electricity*
# SLIME

THIS IS ONE OF THE BEST EXPERIMENTS FOR YOUNGER scientists. It's very messy, and the seemingly risky combination of ooze and electricity makes for a good show.

## You Will Need

- 2 CUPS VEGETABLE OIL
- 2/3 CUP CORNSTARCH
- LARGE DRINKING GLASS
- REFRIGERATOR
- 8-INCH X 8-INCH X 1-INCH STYROFOAM BLOCK
- WOOL SOCK

# METHOD

 Mix the oil and cornstarch in the glass.

 Put this mixture in the refrigerator until it's well chilled.

 Remove from the refrigerator and stir (don't worry if it has separated).

 Let the mixture warm up enough so that it can flow; it will resemble slime at this point.

 When the mixture is ready, rub the Styrofoam block on the wool sock (or on your hair if there's no wool sock handy).

TAKE CARE! THIS IS ONE OF THOSE RARE EXPERIMENTS THAT'S SAFE ENOUGH TO RECOMMEND EVEN TO YOUR KID BROTHER OR SISTER. JUST REMEMBER TO MAKE SURE THAT THE GLASS IS BIG ENOUGH TO HOLD THE OIL-CORNSTARCH MIXTURE.

**6** Tip the container of slime and put the electrically charged Styrofoam about an inch away from it. The slime should seem to stop flowing, and even to gel.

**7** Try wiggling the Styrofoam: Bits of slime might break off and follow it.

**8** You can refrigerate the slime in a sealed container after the experiment.

## The Scientific Excuse

When rubbed, the Styrofoam draws electrons from the wool (or hair), giving the Styrofoam a negative charge. Meanwhile, the oil and cornstarch combine to make a substance known as a colloid. In school we learn that there are three forms of matter: solid, liquid, and gas. But there's actually a fourth kind of matter—a colloid—that is neither a solid nor a liquid, although it has characteristics of both. When the charged Styrofoam nears the colloid, it causes the cornstarch to line up, blocking the flow of the liquid oil. Taking the Styrofoam away lets the mixture behave more a like a normal liquid again.

# Giant Air
# CANNON

**SIMPLE INGREDIENTS, EASY TO MAKE, DRAMATIC RESULTS—** some experiments are almost too good to be true. This air cannon is a lot of fun to make, especially with younger brothers or sisters. You can crank up the "irresponsible" meter dramatically with flour or other non-hazardous powders to add to the effect.

## You Will Need

- 12-INCH X 12-INCH X 12-INCH CARDBOARD BOX
- SCISSORS
- PACKING TAPE
- STRONG PLASTIC SHEET
- FLOUR

*TAKE CARE!* **THIS IS ONE OF THE LEAST RISKY EXPERIMENTS IN THE BOOK.**

## METHOD

**1** Cut off the flaps from one end of the box using the scissors. At the other end, tape the flaps together and cut out a single 6-inch circle.

**2** Reinforce this circular opening with tape.

**3** Tape the plastic sheet over the open end of the box, leaving plenty of slack; allow it to overlap each side by 5 inches before taping it securely.

**4** Pinch the slack plastic sheeting in the middle and then punch it hard to operate the air cannon.

**5** Try putting some flour inside the cannon and then opening fire.

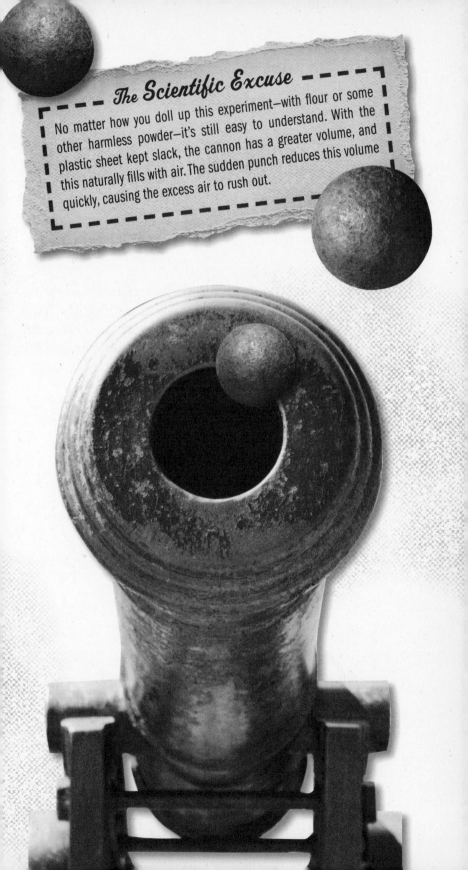

## The Scientific Excuse

No matter how you doll up this experiment—with flour or some other harmless powder—it's still easy to understand. With the plastic sheet kept slack, the cannon has a greater volume, and this naturally fills with air. The sudden punch reduces this volume quickly, causing the excess air to rush out.

# *Burning* ICE

LIGHTING A FIRE WITH A BLOCK OF ice? SURELY THAT'S A contradiction in terms! Try this experiment to see for yourself how the forces of nature can overturn common sense. It's certainly one display you and your audience won't easily forget.

## *You Will Need*

- SAUCEPAN
- WATER
- SHALLOW, EVENLY CURVED PLASTIC BOWL (ABOUT 8 INCHES WIDE)
- ENOUGH ROOM ON A FREEZER
- SHELF FOR THE BOWL
- BLACK CREPE PAPER
- FLAMEPROOF PLATE
- SUNLIGHT

*TAKE CARE!* THERE ARE FEW RISKS TIED IN WITH THIS EXPERIMENT. YOU DON'T NEED TO USE A LARGE PIECE OF PAPER—THE WHOLE POINT IS JUST TO SHOW HOW POWERFUL THE LENS COULD BE. PLUS, THERE'S NO REAL FIRE RISK IF YOU DOUSE THE PAPER WITH WATER AS SOON AS IT CATCHES FIRE.

# METHOD

**1** Boil a saucepan of water for 3–4 minutes and then let it cool to just above room temperature.

**2** Fill the bowl with the previously boiled water.

**3** Carefully place the bowl of water on a shelf in the freezer and allow it to freeze completely.

**4** Scrunch up a small piece of the crepe paper and set it on a flameproof plate.

**5** Remove the ice from the bowl (running a little warm water over the back of the bowl can help to release it).

**6** Hold the ice, which is shaped like a lens, above the paper and direct the sunlight at the paper.

**7** Keep the ice still until the paper ignites.

## The Scientific Excuse

This experiment operates under the same principle as letting a magnifying glass light an object: it concentrates, or refracts, the sunlight and focuses it on the paper. The ice has very little chance of cooling these rays. And boiling the water first is important as a way of "purifying" the lens. Ordinary water has many bubbles inside it: Even the ones too small for us to see can distort the lens and make it less effective.

# Chapter Three

# FOOD *for* THOUGHT

**I**t's amazing to think that just about every branch of science can be studied in the kitchen, using ingredients from the cupboard, refrigerator, pantry, or silverware drawer. Billowing black smoke, flying potato pieces, a mysterious growing hand—these things are the real stuff of science, aren't they? You can eat some of the results, but you might find that others have simply disappeared. All of this adds a wild new twist to the term "domestic science."

**MATCH ALERT!** This experiment involves the use of matches and should only be conducted with a responsible adult present.

# *Bacon* SMOKESCREEN

HERE'S A WAY TO INDULGE YOUR WISH TO ENTER THE WORLD of smoke and mirrors. Smokescreens are popular with scientists young and old, and it's always nice to be able to eat your experiment!

## *You Will Need*

- PACKAGE OF BACON
- FRYING PAN
- 8-INCH X 6-INCH PIECE OF ALUMINUM FOIL, PLUS EXTRA TO SERVE AS THE BASE
- STRING
- MATCHES

*TAKE CARE!* ALTHOUGH THE EXPERIMENT ISN'T DANGEROUS, IT DOES PRODUCE A GREAT DEAL OF SMOKE. NOW THAT, OF COURSE, IS THE WHOLE POINT OF THE EXPERIMENT, BUT REMEMBER TO PLAN AHEAD, TAKING INTO ACCOUNT VENTILATION, WIND SPEED, WHO'S LIKELY TO SEE OR SMELL THE SMOKE, AND SO ON. ALSO REMEMBER TO DO THIS AWAY FROM SMOKE ALARMS!

# METHOD

1. Fry the bacon until it has given off most of its fat in the form of grease (drippings); allow grease to cool.

2. Meanwhile, form a tube with the aluminum foil, sealing one end and keeping the other open.

3. Cut a length of string an inch longer than the height of the tube.

4. Pour the bacon grease into the tube.

5. When the grease has begun to set but is still malleable, feed the string into it so that the extra inch protrudes; it will serve as a wick.

6. Let the grease harden, then remove it from the tube and place it on a nonflammable base (also possibly made from foil).

7. Light the fuse; it will burn like a candle but will emit a thick black smoke.

## The Scientific Excuse

A car without the right fuel mix (gasoline and oxygen) will not "flash burn" efficiently and will burn off the gasoline with far more smoke. This experiment presents a small-scale version of the same thing—this is a mix that scores high on fuel (the bacon grease) and low on oxygen, providing the slow-burning part of things. The impurities in animal fat (particles of meat and bone that burn black) make the smoke very dark.

# POTATO GUN

**THIS EXPERIMENT TAKES THE NOTION OF A FOOD FIGHT** and introduces a note of the "arms race." The basic ammunition is simple enough—the humble potato. But with a little preparation, and some help from Boyle's Law, the potato will "go ballistic"—literally!

## You Will Need

- GOGGLES
- 2 POTATOES
- 4-FOOT LENGTH OF PVC PIPE (1-INCH DIAMETER), AVAILABLE AT MOST HARDWARE STORES
- 5-FOOT WOODEN BROOMSTICK (DIAMETER NARROWER THAN THAT OF THE TUBE)
- RUBBER STOPPER (OPTIONAL)

### The Scientific Excuse

This experiment is an explosive demonstration of Boyle's Law: Pressure increases as volume decreases. Scientifically stated, this means: "Under constant temperature, the volume of a gas is inversely proportional to the total amount of pressure applied." In this experiment, the gas is the air inside the pipe, lodged between the two potato plugs. When you shove the broomstick into the pipe, you push one plug toward the other. This suddenly reduces the volume of the gas, thereby increasing its pressure. Something has to give: The burst of pressure sends the potato plug flying.

# METHOD

**1** Press one end of the pipe down into a potato, so that a plug of potato becomes lodged in the end.

**2** Repeat this process with the other potato in the other end of the pipe so that you have a potato plug at each end.

**3** Put on your goggles. With one hand, hold the pipe with one end pointing away from you— and anything breakable.

**4** Position the broomstick at the closer end of the pipe, just touching the potato plug. (If the broomstick is much narrower than the pipe, add a rubber stopper to the end touching the potato.)

**5** Edge the broomstick slowly down the pipe, pushing one potato plug toward the other. Stop when you are about a third of the way down, and pull the broomstick back.

**6** Now, ram the broomstick back into the pipe very quickly. The plug at the far ("barrel") end will shoot out with great force.

POP!

*TAKE CARE!* **DON'T POINT THE POTATO GUN IN THE DIRECTION OF ANYONE WATCHING—OR TOWARD ANY CHINA OR GLASS! IT'S BETTER, ALL THINGS CONSIDERED TO DO THIS EXPERIMENT OUTSIDE.**

# FRANKENSTEIN'S HAND

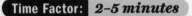

HERE'S A "HANDS-ON" DEMONSTRAtion of a scientific principle that has cropped up elsewhere in this book: the chemical reaction between a comon acid and an equally familiar base. You can give this experiment something of a Halloween flavor by marking the glove with bones, veins, and screws. You can also add a little ketchup at the bottom of the glove—just to raise the gore factor. Your audience will love the special effects as the hand grows and grows.

## You Will Need

- 3 TABLESPOONS VINEGAR
- DRINKING GLASS
- 2 TEASPOONS BAKING SODA
- RUBBER GLOVE

**TAKE CARE!** THIS IS A SAFE EXPERIMENT WITH VERY LITTLE RISK. MAKE SURE THAT THE GLOVE FITS TIGHTLY ON THE GLASS BEFORE YOU DO THE EXPERIMENT; IF IT'S LOOSE, TRY A WIDER-MOUTHED GLASS. YOU MIGHT WANT TO TAKE CARE THAT THE GLOVE DOESN'T INFLATE TOO MUCH, WHICH COULD CAUSE IT TO FLY OFF THE GLASS. AND IN CASE YOU'RE THINKING ABOUT HAVING A LITTLE FUN AT YOUR LITTLE BROTHER OR SISTER'S EXPENSE—SAY, BY TELLING THEM YOU FOUND THIS HAND ON THE SIDEWALK—DON'T COME RUNNING TO US IF YOU GET IN TROUBLE WITH THE PARENTAL UNITS!

# METHOD

1 Pour the vinegar into the glass.

2 Add the baking soda to the inside of the glove. Hold the glove by its wrist and shake the powder into the fingers.

kinda stinks . . .

3 Carefully attach the glove to the top of the glass as shown so there's no gap.

4 Pull the glove upright by its fingertips and shake gently, allowing the baking soda to drop into the glass.

5 Stand back and watch as Frankenstein's hand begins to come alive.

It's alive!

## The Scientific Excuse

Baking soda is a chemical base, which reacts strongly with the acetic acid of the vinegar. One of the by-products of this reaction is carbon dioxide, which increases the pressure inside the glove-glass arrangement. As more gas is produced, the pressure increases further and pushes out the weaker surface (the rubber glove), inflating it gently.

# EGG

## Bungee Jump

**HAVE YOU EVER DONE A BUNGEE JUMP? DOES IT GIVE YOU** the shakes just thinking about it? How about trying a home version of it where the egg does the jumping, but with an added, possibly very messy, ingredient? Be warned: It might leave you quite literally with egg on your face.

## You Will Need

- RULER
- 6 EGGS (ALTHOUGH 1 SHOULD BE ENOUGH)
- SUPPLY OF PENNIES
- PAIR OF PANTYHOSE
- STRONG TAPE
- NEWSPAPER

# METHOD

**1** Choose a spot for the bungee jump: ideally a tree branch outdoors, but it could also work from a ladder. You want the egg to fall to within an inch of your face when you're lying on the ground looking up at it, but no closer.

**2** Get a friend to use the ruler to measure the length from the back of your head to the tip of your nose; your friend should then add the "inch for safety" to this length.

**3** Work out the weight of the egg beforehand to do a test run: Hold the egg in one hand and add pennies to the other until you feel that the coins weigh the same as the egg.

*TAKE CARE!* IF, FOR SOME REASON, YOU'RE DOING THIS INDOORS, MAKE SURE YOU SPREAD OUT SOME OLD NEWSPAPER FOR A LANDING SITE. AND, HEY, IF YOUR MOM FINDS THE EVIDENCE OF SOME "NEAR MISSES" ON THE FLOOR—JUST TELL HER YOU WERE LEARNING ABOUT NEWTONIAN PHYSICS AND THE LAWS OF GRAVITY. THAT SHOULD HELP KEEP THE COMPLAINTS TO A MINIMUM.

**4** Add the "egg's worth" of pennies to a leg of the pantyhose and tape the end of the other leg to the branch or ladder.

**5** Do the test run: Let the pantyhose full of coins fall and check their distance from the ground. They should stop above the ground at exactly the distance that your friend calculated in Step 2. Make any necessary adjustments to where you have tied the pantyhose to the branch or ladder.

**6** Now for the real thing: Call in your audience, settle yourself in place on the ground, and after a suspenseful countdown, let your friend do the drop—this time with the egg.

## The Scientific Excuse

The nylon or other stretchy fabric of the pantyhose has a natural elasticity—a certain force will take it so far before the strength of the fabric pulls it back. The measuring and the test runs might all seem like good fun, but you—or your younger assistants—are actually working out the components of the famous physics equation:

force = mass × acceleration.

Well done, Newton!

# Turning MILK TO STONE

**THERE'S SOMETHING ALMOST MAGICAL IN THE TITLE OF THIS** experiment, but once you've done it and understood what's happened you'll also be reminded of Little Miss Muffet. Regardless of which reference you prefer (maybe none at all), this demonstration scores high on the "kewl" and "awesome" scale.

## You Will Need

- 1½ CUPS SKIM MILK
- MICROWAVE-SAFE MIXING BOWL
- 4 TEASPOONS VINEGAR
- MICROWAVE OVEN
- STRAINER
- EMPTY MILK CONTAINER

*TAKE CARE!* MAKE SURE YOU USE THE MICROWAVE RESPONSIBLY. OTHERWISE, THIS EXPERIMENT IS HAZARD-FREE. (UNLESS WHOEVER POURED THEMSELVES A CUP OF "STONE" DIDN'T APPRECIATE THE HUMOR!)

# METHOD

**1** Pour the milk into the mixing bowl.

**2** Add the vinegar.

**3** Put this mixture in the microwave and cook it on high for 1 minute.

**4** Remove it from the microwave to find it now composed of a solid and a liquid.

**5** Strain off the liquid.

**6** Let the solid cool and then form it into little shapes, which will harden as they cool.

**7** Put the shapes back into the empty milk container, and put the container in the refrigerator. Next time someone goes for a nice refreshing cup of milk, won't they be surprised to find weird hard little shapes inside instead?

## The Scientific Excuse

The acid in the vinegar separates the curd (the semi-solid element) from the whey (the liquid) in the milk. The protein in the curd accounts for its rubbery quality—in fact, some of the earliest plastics were produced in a variation of this experiment.

# IRON
## Breakfast Cereal

NO WONDER IT WAS SO CRUNCHY! ACTUALLY, CEREAL manufacturers have long played a part in providing us with essential minerals in our daily breakfast. Maybe this experiment could be a springboard to more lucrative exploits: "There's gold in them thar cornflakes!" Pump up the "irresponsibility" meter by asking your dad if he'll have a teaspoon of cereal. Only have him wait until after you've performed the experiment, and offer him the end result. He may never look at cereal in the same way again!

## You Will Need

- MAGNET TAPE
- TONGUE DEPRESSOR
- 2 ZIPLOCK SANDWICH BAGS
- SINGLE PORTION OF "FORTIFIED" BREAKFAST CEREAL (CHECK INGREDIENTS TO MAKE SURE IT CONTAINS IRON)
- NONMETAL MIXING BOWL (1 PINT MINIMUM CAPACITY)
- WATER

*TAKE CARE!* THERE'S NO RISK WITH THIS EXPERIMENT, BUT BE PATIENT IN THE STIRRING. TEN MINUTES IS A LONG TIME BUT WE'RE TALKING ABOUT SMALL AMOUNTS OF IRON AND ANY LESS STIRRING WOULDN'T BE SUCCESSFUL.

# METHOD

**1** Attach the magnet tape to one end of the tongue depressor and seal it in one of the sandwich bags.

**2** Put the cereal in the other sandwich bag and crush it.

**3** Pour the crushed cereal into the mixing bowl and add water to cover.

**4** Keeping it within the sandwich bag, use the now-magnetic tongue depressor to stir the cereal for 10 minutes.

**5** Remove the stirring device from the mixing bowl and observe the tiny metal filings on the outside of it.

## The Scientific Excuse

Humans need iron and other minerals in their daily diet. Many breakfast cereals are "fortified" to help us meet this dietary requirement. Normally we wouldn't give this an extra thought, but after seeing the results of the experiment, it all seems a little clearer—if perhaps a little less tasty. These iron filings are oxidized (broken down further) in the stomach and absorbed in the small intestine. If all the iron in your body could be extracted, you'd have enough to make a couple of small nails.

# The ELECTRIC SPOON

WE'VE ALL HEARD COOKS CRY OUT WHEN THEY'VE BEEN following a recipe: "Oh, dear! I've mixed the ingredients too soon: They were meant to be separate at this stage." Imagine if you could turn back the clock and pick the mixture apart bit by bit. Imagine further that you could do this with salt and pepper. Impossible? Read on and think again!

## You Will Need

- 1 TEASPOON TABLE SALT
- 1 TEASPOON GROUND BLACK PEPPER
- PLASTIC SPOON
- WOOL SOCK (YOUR HAIR WILL DO IF THERE'S NO WOOL SOCK HANDY)
- PIECE OF PAPER (OPTIONAL)

*TAKE CARE!* THE PEPPER JUMPS UP FIRST BECAUSE IT'S LIGHTER THAN THE SALT. THAT'S WHY LOWERING THE SPOON SLOWLY IS SO IMPORTANT: TOO FAST AND THE SALT AND PEPPER WOULD JUMP UP TOGETHER. IF YOU WANT TO COMPLETE THE "TIDYING UP" AFTER ALL THE PEPPER HAS BEEN REMOVED, SIMPLY CARRY ON WITH THE PROCESS, MOVING THE SPOON A BIT LOWER.

# METHOD

 Mix the salt and pepper on a smooth, dry surface.

 Rub the spoon vigorously against the wool sock (or your hair).

 Slowly and very carefully lower the spoon toward the salt-pepper mixture.

4. When it's an inch or two from the surface, the pepper will jump up, grain by grain, to the spoon's surface.

 Stop the experiment here if you simply want to show how it works. To complete the separation, continue with Steps 6 and 7.

6. Slide a piece of paper under the spoon and shake the pepper grains onto it.

7. Rub the spoon against the sock again and repeat until all the pepper has "jumped" to the spoon and only salt remains.

## The Scientific Excuse

Several experiments in this book—including this one—depend on building an electrical flow by rubbing plastic or another substance against wool. As the negatively charged plastic spoon is lowered, it charges the salt and pepper by a process called induction. The nearest surface of the salt and pepper gains a positive charge and the far side a negative. Since "opposites attract," the grains of pepper and salt jump toward the spoon.

# "KICK-START"

**MOST IRRESPONSIBLE EXPERIMENTS TRIGGER SATISFYING** bangs, smells, oozes, and explosions. Not many produce anything you'd like to eat. This experiment is an exception. It's fun, reckless, and runs the risk of being very, very messy—but it produces some of the best homemade ice cream you'll ever taste.

Don't touc my cone!

# ICE CREAM

## *You Will Need*

- 1 CUP HEAVY CREAM
- 1 CUP WHOLE MILK
- 6 TABLESPOONS WHITE SUGAR
- 2 TABLESPOONS VANILLA EXTRACT
- CLEAN, EMPTY COFFEE CAN AND ITS PLASTIC LID (OR A LIDDED PLASTIC CONTAINER OF THE SAME SIZE)
- 4-GALLON PLASTIC BUCKET WITH LID
- LARGE BAG OF ICE (AVAILABLE FROM MOST SUPERMARKETS)
- A GENEROUS 3/4 (MORE LIKE 4/5) CUP ROCK SALT
- SPOON TO EAT ICE CREAM (MORE THAN ONE IF YOU ARE TEMPTED TO SHARE THE RESULT)
- DUCT TAPE OR PACKING TAPE

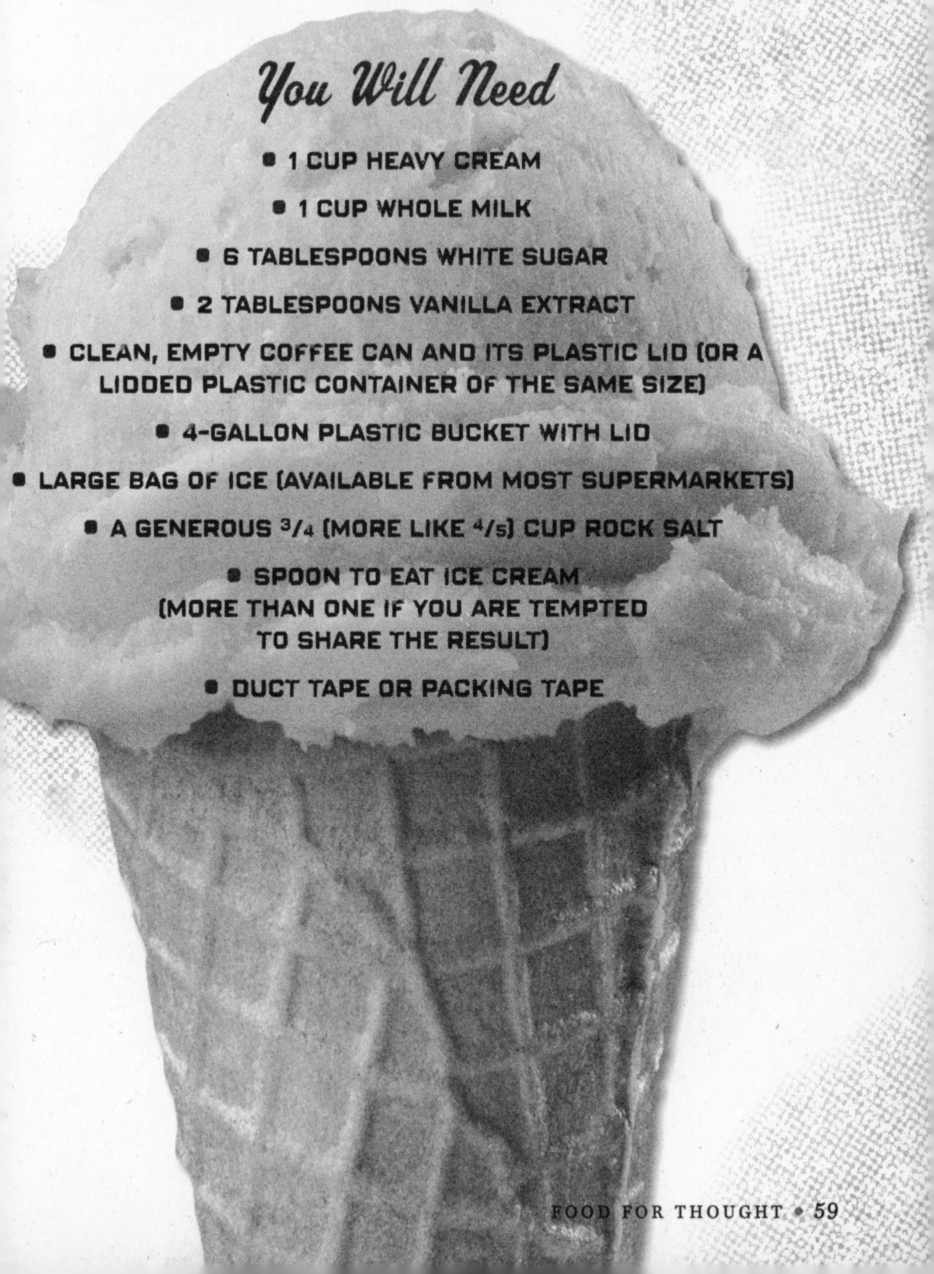

# METHOD

 **1** Mix the cream, milk, sugar, and vanilla in the coffee can. It should fill the can no more than halfway.

**2** Put the lid on the coffee can, tape it shut, and put it in the large bucket.

**3** Add a 4-inch layer of ice to the bucket in the space around the coffee can, and then sprinkle the rock salt in the same area.

**4** Fill the rest of the bucket with ice and snap the plastic lid onto it; tape it shut.

*TAKE CARE!* HELPERS—ESPECIALLY YOUNGER ONES—HAVE A HABIT OF BECOMING OVERZEALOUS DURING THE "KICK AND ROLL THE BUCKET" PHASE OF THIS EXPERIMENT. IT'S PROBABLY A GOOD IDEA TO TAPE BOTH LIDS (COFFEE CAN AND BUCKET) FIRMLY IN PLACE BEFOREHAND.

**5** Now, get your helpers to kick and roll the bucket around for about 10 minutes.

**6** Open the bucket, then remove and open the coffee can. A layer of frozen ice cream will line the inside of the can. Stir this into the chilled inner liquid to get the right consistency.

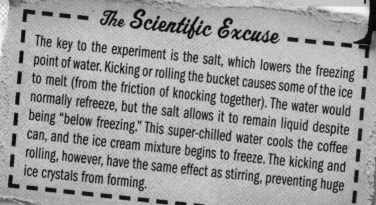

### The Scientific Excuse

The key to the experiment is the salt, which lowers the freezing point of water. Kicking or rolling the bucket causes some of the ice to melt (from the friction of knocking together). The water would normally refreeze, but the salt allows it to remain liquid despite being "below freezing." This super-chilled water cools the coffee can, and the ice cream mixture begins to freeze. The kicking and rolling, however, have the same effect as stirring, preventing huge ice crystals from forming.

# Reinforced RICE

**THIS WONDERFUL, COUNTERINTUITIVE** experiment can be performed in a matter of a few seconds, especially if you keep your rice in the right type of jar. There's something primal and moving about it—which might explain why unscrupulous sorcerers in days long past would claim magic powers when performing this trick.

## You Will Need

- 1-PINT PLASTIC JAR
- 2 POUNDS OF UNCOOKED RICE (OR ENOUGH TO FILL THE JAR)
- SHARP KNIFE

*TAKE CARE!* ANY KNIFE WIELDING SHOULD BE ATTEMPT-ED ONLY UNDER THE SUPERVISION OF AN ADULT. MAKE SURE THAT YOUNGER OBSERVERS STAND WELL BACK. OTHERWISE, THIS EXPERIMENT IS SAFE.

# METHOD

 Fill the jar with the rice.

 Repeatedly plunge the knife *halfway* into the rice, preferably at an angle.

 Jab the knife *fully* into the rice.

 Pull straight up on the knife and it will mysteriously carry the jar of rice with it.

## The Scientific Excuse

The force of pressure of thousands of grains of rice can overcome the force of gravity. Those preliminary "stabs" of the rice serve to settle it in tightly. The knife is sharp enough to be jabbed into this network of pressure, but the rice settles back in from all sides to hold the knife in place.

# EGGS IN THE NUDE

**SOME EXPERIMENTS COME INTO THEIR OWN ONLY AFTER** you've done a little behind-the-scenes groundwork beforehand. If you're planning on demonstrating this experiment to an audience, you might want to adopt this approach, since you'll need a good two days' worth of preparation. (And it takes another day or two to get the real payoff.) The experiment calls for two eggs, although you should need only one. The extra one is held in reserve, since these "eggs in the nude" are very delicate without their shells.

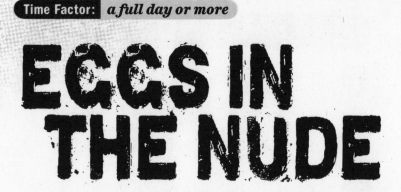

Can't a guy get a little privacy around here?

But I'm on the guest list...

## You Will Need

- 2 EGGS
- 2-PINT PLASTIC MIXING BOWL WITH LID
- 2 PINTS VINEGAR
- REFRIGERATED
- WOODEN SPOON
- COFFEE MUG
- $5/8$ CUP CORN SYRUP

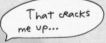

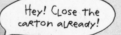

# METHOD

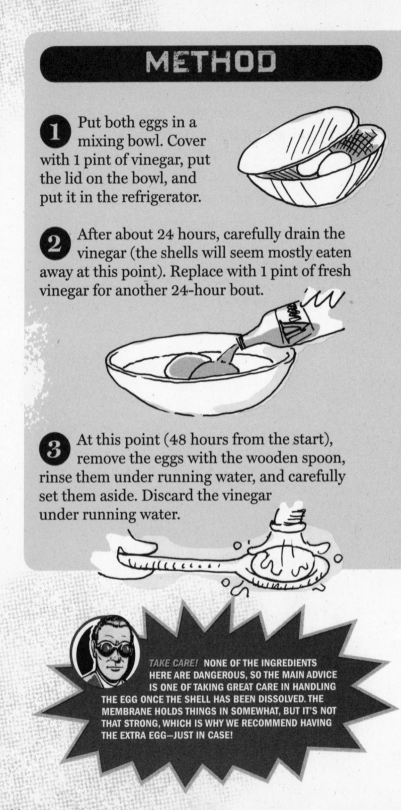

**1** Put both eggs in a mixing bowl. Cover with 1 pint of vinegar, put the lid on the bowl, and put it in the refrigerator.

**2** After about 24 hours, carefully drain the vinegar (the shells will seem mostly eaten away at this point). Replace with 1 pint of fresh vinegar for another 24-hour bout.

**3** At this point (48 hours from the start), remove the eggs with the wooden spoon, rinse them under running water, and carefully set them aside. Discard the vinegar under running water.

*TAKE CARE!* NONE OF THE INGREDIENTS HERE ARE DANGEROUS, SO THE MAIN ADVICE IS ONE OF TAKING GREAT CARE IN HANDLING THE EGG ONCE THE SHELL HAS BEEN DISSOLVED. THE MEMBRANE HOLDS THINGS IN SOMEWHAT, BUT IT'S NOT THAT STRONG, WHICH IS WHY WE RECOMMEND HAVING THE EXTRA EGG—JUST IN CASE!

**4** Show your audience one of the eggs, holding it carefully in the wooden spoon, and place it in the coffee mug. Then cover it with the corn syrup.

**5** After another 24 hours, extract the egg with the wooden spoon and notice how flabby it has become.

**6** Now discard the corn syrup, rinse the mug, and put the egg back in, covered this time with water.

**7** After 24 hours (48 hours from Step 3) you'll see that the egg is looking healthier again.

Let's Jog!

## The Scientific Excuse

There are a few things going on here, all having to do with chemistry. To remove the shell and make the eggs "nude," you immersed them in vinegar. The acetic acid of the vinegar ate away the sodium-calcium carbonate crystals of the shell, leaving only the rubbery membrane surrounding the egg. That membrane is slightly permeable, allowing water to move from an area of higher concentration (the egg white, for example, is about 90 percent water) to one of lower concentration (corn syrup is about 25 percent water). When you replace the corn syrup in the coffee mug with water, you reverse this process.

# *Marshmallows* ON STEROIDS?

**JUST IN CASE YOU'VE SPENT FOUR DAYS ON THE LAST EXPERI-**ment tending to your "eggs in the nude," we thought you'd like a real quickie. This experiment is probably one of the quickest and easiest in the book, provided you have a vacuum storage jar (often sold for coffee).

## You Will Need

- 2-PINT STORAGE JAR WITH VACUUM PUMP
- MARSHMALLOWS (FULL-SIZE FLUFFY VARIETY)

*TAKE CARE!* WHAT CAN GO WRONG WITH MARSHMALLOWS, FOR GOODNESS' SAKE? NOTHING IRRESPONSIBLE HERE, REALLY, UNLESS YOU DECIDE TO WOLF DOWN ALL THE MARSHMALLOWS AFTER YOU'VE FINISHED THE EXPERIMENT. THIS COULD BE HAZARDOUS IF YOU DO THIS RIGHT BEFORE DINNER AND YOUR MOM FINDS OUT.

## METHOD

**1** Fill the jar with marshmallows, but don't pack them in tightly.

**2** Cover the jar and pump it to remove as much air as you can.

**3** Examine the marshmallows, which should appear much puffier than before.

**4** Release the pump and observe as the marshmallows return to their original size.

### The Scientific Excuse

Easy, if still dramatic and amusing. Pumping the air out of the container reduces the air pressure inside. When you consider that marshmallows are mainly air bubbles, with some linking solids, you can see how the air in the bubbles would expand to fill the less pressurized air around them. The marshmallow "solids" (the non-bubble bits) are elastic enough to expand with the bubbles. When you release the pump, the marshmallows shrink back to normal.

# *Vanishing* MILK

**SEVERAL OF THE EXPERIMENTS IN THIS BOOK ARE DRAMATIC** enough to qualify as magic tricks. This is one of them. Your audience will be dumbfounded as you pour a healthy glass of milk and then make to pour it back into the jug, undrunk. But it's gone! What happened? Is science to blame?

## You Will Need

- RUBBER GLOVES
- GOGGLES
- DISPOSABLE DIAPER
- SHARP KNIFE
- $1/2$-TEASPOON MEASURING SPOON
- SEMIOPAQUE DRINKING GLASS
- 2 CUPS MILK
- 2-PINT CLEAR GLASS PITCHER

# METHOD

**1** Wearing gloves and goggles, cut open the center of a disposable diaper with a sharp knife.

**2** Scoop out ½ teaspoon of the powder inside the diaper (known as sodium polyacrylate) and put it in the semiopaque drinking glass.

**3** Pour the milk into the pitcher. You are now ready to perform the trick for your public.

**4** Hold the drinking glass out before you in one hand and the full pitcher of milk in the other. Here's your chance to show off your talents as a magician: Talk it up for your audience!

*TAKE CARE!* SODIUM POLYACRYLATE CAN IRRITATE THE EYES AND NOSTRILS, SO TAKE CARE WHEN YOU ARE DEALING WITH IT. TRY TO USE GOGGLES AND NOT TO INHALE ANY OF IT. KEEP IT WELL AWAY FROM ANYONE IN YOUR AUDIENCE. ALSO MAKE SURE YOU WEAR GLOVES. AS FOR PRACTICAL ADVICE, THIS EXPERIMENT WORKS BETTER AS A TRICK IF YOU DON'T USE A CLEAR GLASS. THAT WAY, YOUR AUDIENCE WON'T HAVE A CHANCE TO NOTICE THE MILKY GEL LEFT AT THE BOTTOM OF THE GLASS. LAST, DISPOSE OF THE SODIUM POLYACRYLATE IN THE GARBAGE—NOT THE SINK—SINCE IT MIGHT CLOG UP YOUR DRAIN.

**5** Pour some milk from the pitcher into the drinking glass.

**6** Pretend you're about to drink the milk, but then tell your audience that you've changed your mind. You're not thirsty after all, so you're going to pour the milk back into the pitcher. Try to pour the milk from the glass into the pitcher. None will come out!

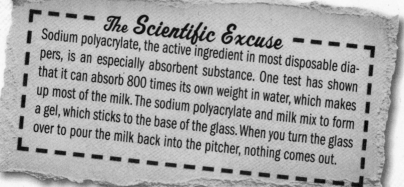

## The Scientific Excuse

Sodium polyacrylate, the active ingredient in most disposable diapers, is an especially absorbent substance. One test has shown that it can absorb 800 times its own weight in water, which makes up most of the milk. The sodium polyacrylate and milk mix to form a gel, which sticks to the base of the glass. When you turn the glass over to pour the milk back into the pitcher, nothing comes out.

# STRAW THROUGH A POTATO?

**WE'VE ALL HEARD ABOUT THE SAVAGE FORCE OF A TORNADO.** Its 300 mile-per-hour winds are strong enough to drive a piece of straw clear through a telephone pole. So you can imagine that if you left a drinking straw near a potato as a tornado approached, you might return to find the potato skewered by the straw. But can you imagine getting the same result by hand? Read on, and see how you can do it.

## You Will Need

- GARDENING GLOVE (LEFT GLOVE IF YOU'RE RIGHT-HANDED OR VICE VERSA)
- UNCOOKED POTATO
- RIGID (NON-BENDY) DRINKING STRAW

*TAKE CARE!* THIS IS A RELATIVELY LOW-RISK EXPERIMENT, ALTHOUGH THE SAME COMBINATION OF STRENGTH AND SHARPNESS OF THE STRAW COULD LEAD TO A HAND INJURY IF YOUR AIM ISN'T UP TO SCRATCH. (THAT'S WHY YOU SHOULD USE THE GARDENING GLOVE.)

# METHOD

**1** Put the glove on one hand.

**2** Hold the potato (lengthwise vertically) with the gloved hand, pinching it between your thumb and index finger.

**3** Holding the potato steady, pick up the straw (holding it in the middle), and line it up with the potato.

**4** Slowly draw the straw back, then stab the straw quickly into the potato.

**5** If you're quick enough—and the straw is strong enough—you'll stab it right through the potato.

ouch!

## The *Scientific Excuse*

The cylindrical shape of the straw gives it surprising strength along its length, although it remains weak and flexible crossways. That strength, coupled with the narrowness and sharpness of its edge, gives the straw a good chance of making it through the potato with ease. Some people might see your thumb over one end of the straw as you push and decide that it's all due to air pressure. That's a nice try, but not the reason—and you can prove it by doing the experiment again with your thumb well away from the open end of the straw.

# Give Peas
# A CHANCE

**THIS LITTLE GEM OF AN EXPERIMENT SCORES HIGH ON THE** "scientific excuse" side of the equation, giving you a real chance to demonstrate—or learn more about—plants and how they nourish themselves. Well, there's the justification out of the way. The experiment also offers a chance to capitalize on the spooky *plip-plop* that others (those who aren't in on the experiment) will find so puzzling and unsettling. Try different positions in the kitchen—or elsewhere—to hide the setup. You can also add a bit of scrunched-up foil to the baking sheet for a bit of audio variety. With their seeming patience, the peas appear to be lining up to drop out of the glass.

## You Will Need

- THIN METAL BAKING SHEET OR LID (ABOUT 8–10 INCHES WIDE, EITHER SQUARE OR CIRCULAR)
- WIDE-MOUTH (2–3 INCHES) DRINKING GLASS WITH A HEAVY BASE
- WINEGLASS
- DRIED PEAS (ENOUGH TO FILL THE WINEGLASS)
- WATER

*TAKE CARE!* **MAKE SURE YOU DON'T LEAVE THIS ARRANGEMENT TOO CLOSE TO THE EDGE OF A COUNTER OR ON AN UNSTEADY SURFACE.**

# METHOD

**1** Place the baking sheet or lid on top of the wide-mouthed drinking glass.

Geronimo!

**2** Put the wineglass on top of the baking sheet or lid.

**3** Fill the wineglass to overflowing with dried peas.

**4** Add water to come right up to the brim of the wineglass.

**5** Slowly, over the course of the next few hours, the peas will fill with water and begin falling—with a spooky *plink*—onto the baking sheet or lid.

PLINK

PLINK

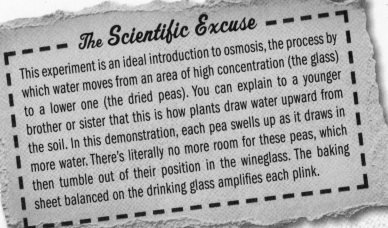

## The Scientific Excuse

This experiment is an ideal introduction to osmosis, the process by which water moves from an area of high concentration (the glass) to a lower one (the dried peas). You can explain to a younger brother or sister that this is how plants draw water upward from the soil. In this demonstration, each pea swells up as it draws in more water. There's literally no more room for these peas, which then tumble out of their position in the wineglass. The baking sheet balanced on the drinking glass amplifies each plink.

# EGG
## *in a Bottle*

**HERE'S ANOTHER TAKE ON THE** scientific principle of creating a vacuum. In this case, a hard-boiled egg gets sucked into a bottle when a match goes out. If this is all getting a bit easy, then try the raw egg variation (see Step 5).

*TAKE CARE!* **MAKE SURE YOU LEAVE THE MATCH BURNING FOR AS LONG AS POSSIBLE BEFORE PUTTING THE EGG ON THE BOTTLE. THE LONGER THE MATCH BURNS, THE HOTTER THE AIR INSIDE BECOMES AND THE GREATER THE DIFFERENCE BETWEEN THE AIR PRESSURES INSIDE AND OUT.**

## *You Will Need*

- PEELED HARD-BOILED EGG
- OLD-FASHIONED 1-PINT GLASS MILK BOTTLE
- MATCHES (LONG KITCHEN MATCHES ARE BEST)
- UNCOOKED EGG (OPTIONAL)
- 3/4 CUP VINEGAR (OPTIONAL)

# METHOD

**1** Have a couple of practice runs resting the egg narrow side down on the lip of the milk bottle.

**2** Light a match and then drop it into the bottle.

**3** When the match has almost burned out (judge by the length of the unburned portion), place the egg back on top of the bottle.

**4** Watch as the egg seems to be sucked into the bottle.

PLOP!

**5** Some people have managed to get the same effect with an uncooked egg in the shell that they first soaked in vinegar for a few hours. (The vinegar softens the shell.)

## The Scientific Excuse

The explanation is pretty simple: The match warms the air, which then expands (some of it escapes) and becomes less dense. Putting the egg on the bottle snuffs out the fire because there is no oxygen supply left. The egg rests between normal air pressure (pushing it down) and weaker air pressure from inside (pushing up against it). No contest—the downward pressure wins the day.

# Sandwich
# IN A JAR

**YOU KNOW HOW IT IS: SOMETIMES YOU DON'T LIKE THE** bread in your sandwich but you just love the gooey filling. Wouldn't it be great to be able to get rid of those two stale slices of bread and replace them with different—spreadable—layers? You could even store it in a jar!

## You Will Need

- 3 TABLESPOONS WATER
- 3 TABLESPOONS COOKING OIL
- 3 TABLESPOONS HONEY
- GLASS MAYONNAISE JAR WITH A LID OR CORK

# METHOD

**1** Pour the water, oil, and honey into the jar.

**2** Cover the jar. Within a few minutes, the "sandwich" will form before your eyes: The liquids separate into 3 distinct layers.

*TAKE CARE!* **YOU'D BETTER NOT TAKE THE SANDWICH IDEA TOO FAR AND MAKE ANYONE EAT IT! SERIOUSLY. OR NOT.**

## The Scientific Excuse

This is all about density (the amount something weighs in a particular volume). The volume (3 tablespoons) remains the same in this experiment, so the densest liquid, the honey, settles at the bottom. The oil is denser than the water, so it settles in the middle, leaving the clear water layer at the top.

# SUPER SALT!

**WE COOK WITH IT, SPRINKLE IT ON FRIES AND POPCORN,** and sometimes preserve food with it. But using salt as a defense mechanism seems to be stretching it a bit. Or does it? Maybe there's more to those little crystals than we ever imagined.

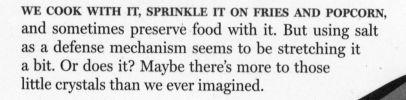

## You Will Need

- SCISSORS
- PIECE OF WAX PAPER
- RUBBER BANDS OR MASKING TAPE
- CARDBOARD TUBE FROM A ROLL OF PAPER TOWELS OR ALUMINUM FOIL)
- BROOMSTICK OR WOODEN DOWEL (NARROW ENOUGH TO FIT INSIDE THE CARDBOARD TUBE)
- ½ CUP TABLE SALT

# METHOD

**1** Cut 2 squares of wax paper, each 6 inches x 6 inches.

**2** Use a rubber band or masking tape to attach one wax paper square to one end of the tube. (It should be spread taut over the end like the top of a drum.)

**3** Feed the broomstick or dowel into the open end and push it all the way through; note how easily it breaks through the paper.

Rip

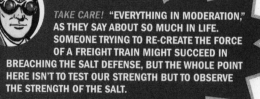

*TAKE CARE!* "EVERYTHING IN MODERATION," AS THEY SAY ABOUT SO MUCH IN LIFE. SOMEONE TRYING TO RE-CREATE THE FORCE OF A FREIGHT TRAIN MIGHT SUCCEED IN BREACHING THE SALT DEFENSE, BUT THE WHOLE POINT HERE ISN'T TO TEST OUR STRENGTH BUT TO OBSERVE THE STRENGTH OF THE SALT.

**4** Replace the torn paper with the second square, securing, it as before.

**5** Now fill the tube with about 3 to 4 inches of salt.

**6** Plunge the broomstick through again. Wait for the salt to spray out . . . but maybe it won't!

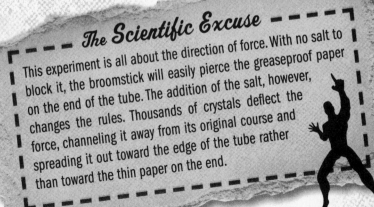

### The Scientific Excuse

This experiment is all about the direction of force. With no salt to block it, the broomstick will easily pierce the greaseproof paper on the end of the tube. The addition of the salt, however, changes the rules. Thousands of crystals deflect the force, channeling it away from its original course and spreading it out toward the edge of the tube rather than toward the thin paper on the end.

# Carrot
# FIRST AID

**WOULDN'T IT BE WONDERFUL TO BE ABLE TO GIVE THE** "kiss of life" to wilted, droopy vegetables? This experiment gives you the chance to do just that, giving a limp carrot the chance to "stand up and be counted" once more—or at least to feel a little more solid.

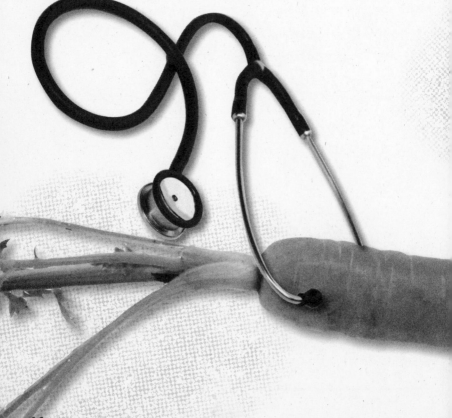

## *You Will Need*

- 8–10-OUNCE CLEAR DRINKING GLASS
- WATER
- KNIFE
- GOOD-SIZE CARROT THAT HAS BECOME LIMP
- CLEAR PLASTIC DRINKING STRAW (CUT DOWN TO 1½ INCHES)
- MODELING CLAY
- 4 TOOTHPICKS
- 1 TEASPOON WATER
- 1 TEASPOON WHITE SUGAR
- SMALL CUP

# METHOD

 Fill the glass about three quarters full of water.

 Using a small knife, hollow out the top of the carrot, about ⅜ inch wide by ½ inch deep.

 Set the straw into this hole leaving about an inch sticking out; seal the edge with modeling clay.

 Stick the toothpicks at equal distances into the sides of the carrot near its top.

 Submerge the carrot in the water, letting the toothpicks rest on the rim of the glass so that the carrot top is still above the water.

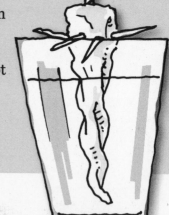

 *TAKE CARE!* **THERE'S NO DANGER INHERENT IN THIS EXPERIMENT. MAKE SURE, THOUGH, TO USE A SUGAR SOLUTION IN THE STRAW: ORDINARY WATER MIGHT EVAPORATE.**

**6** Mix the sugar and the water in the small cup and fill the straw (which juts out from the carrot) about halfway.

**7** Observe the carrot in an hour or two: The water level in the straw should have risen and the carrot should be a lot firmer again.

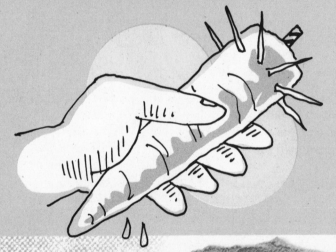

## The Scientific Excuse

This experiment is all about the process called osmosis. Water passes through plant-cell walls as it moves from an area of high concentration (of water) to an area of lower concentration. In this case, the carrot has become limp because it has lost much of the water that gave it support. While in the glass, it absorbs water from its surroundings, becoming more rigid again. In a growing carrot, some of this water would be channeled upward through the top of the orange bit; the addition of the straw (as a sort of gauge) shows how this water level rises.

RAISE "LIVE" Dancing Mothballs!

Teach them:
WALTZ · BALLET · DISCO · BREAK DANCE · HULA · FUNKY · OLD SKOOL... any dance "style" you can think of!

MOTH-BALL DANCING MADE EASY

# Chapter Four

# HOW MOVING!

**C**an you remember Sir Isaac Newton's first law of motion? His second? His third? Don't worry if you can't, because you'll be demonstrating some of them yourself if you carry out some of the following experiments. Everyone loves a chance to build something that rolls, flies, hovers, or blasts off. And to do that in the cause of science—with an eager audience cheering you on—well, that's a little bit of heaven.

# ANTIGRAVITY WATER

**WE'RE ALL AWARE—EVEN UNCONSCIOUSLY—OF THE FORCES** of motion that govern the world around us. Most of us have slid toward the side of a car as it rounded a corner. Maybe we've even leaned into a curve as we've sped on our bikes. Here's a chance to get to the root of that "force of nature." Give it a whirl!

## You Will Need

- HOLE PUNCH
- 7-INCH X 7-INCH SQUARE OF STRONG CARDBOARD
- TWO 3-FOOT-LONG PIECES OF STRING
- PLASTIC OR STYROFOAM CUP
- WATER
- SOME COINS (OPTIONAL)

*TAKE CARE!* THE RISKS HERE ARE PRETTY OBVIOUS, SO YOU SHOULD DO THIS EXPERIMENT OUTDOORS, WHERE THERE'S NO NEED FOR A CLEANUP OR PUBLIC HEARING IF THINGS GO A LITTLE WRONG. AND IF YOU'RE REALLY AFRAID OF GETTING WET, TRY USING A FEW COINS IN THE CUP INSTEAD OF WATER. ONCE YOU'VE GOTTEN THE TRICK TO WORK WITH THE COINS, MOVE ON TO WATER. ONCE YOU'VE MASTERED THE TRICK WITH WATER, MOVE ON TO SOMETHING LIKE CRANBERRY OR TOMATO JUICE—ANYTHING YOUR MOM KNOWS WILL STAIN—AND PERFORM THE EXPERIMENT WHILE SHE WATCHES. HOPEFULLY—FOR YOUR SAKE—ALL YOUR PRACTICE WILL HAVE PAID OFF. IF NOT, DON'T COME CRYING TO US.

**1** Punch a hole about an inch in from each corner of the cardboard.

**2** Feed one end of a piece of string through one hole and the other end of the string up through the diagonally opposite hole.

**3** Repeat Step 2 with the other piece of string so that you have formed a string X at the base of the cardboard. Place the cardboard on a flat surface.

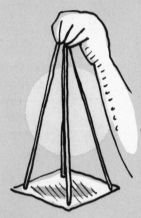

**4** Ensure that the 4 upward-leading strings are the same length, then tie them together so that you can pick up the cardboard "tray" evenly by holding the knot and lifting.

**5** Fill the cup halfway with water and place it in the center of the tray.

**6** Holding the tray by the knot, lift it, and then whirl it around. None of the water should spill out, even when you whirl it in a vertical "orbit."

**7** While still whirling vertically, slow the speed down carefully and pluck the cup from the tray before it can fall off. If you've got the knack, none of the water will have spilled in the experiment. If you don't have the knack, water will have spilled over everything, so try and try again.

## The Scientific Excuse

You have just been demonstrating Newton's first law of motion: "An object in motion will remain in motion unless acted upon by an external and unbalanced force." In this case, swinging the cup sends its contents outward. The tension of the string exerts the "external force," causing the cup to move in a circular path. The water, however, continues to try to move in a linear (straight) path, so it is pushed against the base of the cup. The inward movement of the cup is called centripetal force.

# *Film Canister*
# ROCKET

**HARNESS THE POWERS OF CHEMISTRY AND CALL IN THE AID** of Sir Isaac Newton to send your homemade rocket . . . well, not quite into orbit—but at least zooming off its kitchen launching pad. This experiment can be a group effort from start to finish, from the cutting of the fuselage to providing the voice for the final countdown.

## *You Will Need*

- SCISSORS
- 2–3 SHEETS OF CONSTRUCTION PAPER (LIGHTWEIGHT)
- FILM CANISTER WITH CLICK-SHUT LID
- TAPE
- GLUE
- TEASPOON
- 3 TEASPOONS LEMON JUICE (PER FLIGHT)
- SEVERAL SHEETS OF TOILET PAPER
- 1 TEASPOON BAKING SODA (PER FLIGHT)

*TAKE CARE!* **MAKE SURE YOUR LAUNCH SITE IS SOMEWHERE OUTDOORS—OR AT THE VERY LEAST ON A FLOOR THAT WON'T BE STAINED EASILY. THE TIMING OF THE LAUNCH (ONCE THE INGREDIENTS ARE INSIDE) CAN BE A LITTLE HARD TO PREDICT, SO TAKE CARE NOT TO STAND DIRECTLY ABOVE IT. THE CHEMISTRY BEHIND THE PROPULSION IS FAIL-SAFE, SO IF YOUR ROCKET FAILS TO LAUNCH, EXAMINE IT TO SEE WHETHER IT'S TOO HEAVY. IF SO, MODIFY IT BY REDUCING THE SIZE OF ITS COMPONENTS OR THE AMOUNT OF TAPE OR GLUE USED, THEN SEE IF IT WORKS.**

# METHOD

**1** Cut a piece of construction paper to about 5 inches x 2½ inches: This piece will become the fuselage.

**2** Lay the long end of this piece of paper lengthwise to and flush with the open end of the canister and tape it on, keeping the open end clear of tape. (Throughout construction, go easy with the glue to minimize weight.)

**3** Roll this paper taut around the canister and tape it to the cylinder (it overlaps a bit). One end of the paper cylinder should be flush with the open end of the canister and the other end should extend past the closed end.

**4** Cut a 1½-inch-diameter circle from more construction paper, and then cut out a wedge from the circle that's about one eighth of the circle. Tape shut the wedge-shaped opening in the larger piece that you are left with: This will be the nose cone.

**5** Glue the nose cone to the forward end of the cylinder.

**6** Cut 3 triangles to form old-fashioned "fins" for the base of the rocket. Fold each slightly to create a narrow flap and glue each flap at equal distances on the sides at the base of the rocket.

**7** Hold the rocket upside down. Pour the lemon juice into the film canister part of the rocket.

**8** Stretch a piece of toilet paper over the opening. Pinch it to the edges of the canister so it is held lightly across the opening (with some slack—but not touching the lemon juice).

**9** Pour the baking soda into the slackened paper and—still holding the rocket upside down—snap on the lid. Trim off any excess paper.

**10** Slowly turn over the rocket and place it on the prepared launch site. Stand back and wait: Takeoff is usually within 20 seconds.

## The Scientific Excuse

The reaction between the lemon juice (an acid) and the baking soda (a base) produces carbon dioxide. This gas builds up pressure inside the canister until it blows the lid off the bottom. That's where Newton's third law of motion ("For every action there is an opposite and equal reaction") comes into play. The canister is blown upward with a force equivalent to the one that blew the lid down. Liftoff!

# TENNIS BALL

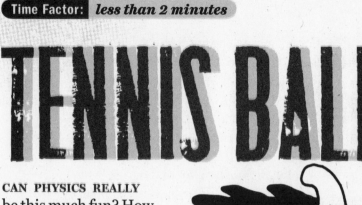

**CAN PHYSICS REALLY** be this much fun? How in the world can you manage to bounce the tennis ball *that* high? You might think of a career in physics after you've done this simple experiment a few times. You'll need three things to make it work well: a steady hand, a hard surface (for a good bounce), and space. It's best performed outdoors on a concrete surface, maybe on a driveway or at a playground.

## You Will Need

- BASKETBALL (A SOCCER BALL OR VOLLEYBALL WILL WORK, BUT NOT AS DRAMATICALLY)
- TENNIS BALL
- GOLF BALL (OPTIONAL)
- PING-PONG BALL (OPTIONAL)
- CARDBOARD TUBE (OPTIONAL)

# MOON BOUNCE

## METHOD

**1** Hold the basketball out at chest height and drop it. Note how high it bounces.

**2** Repeat with the tennis ball.

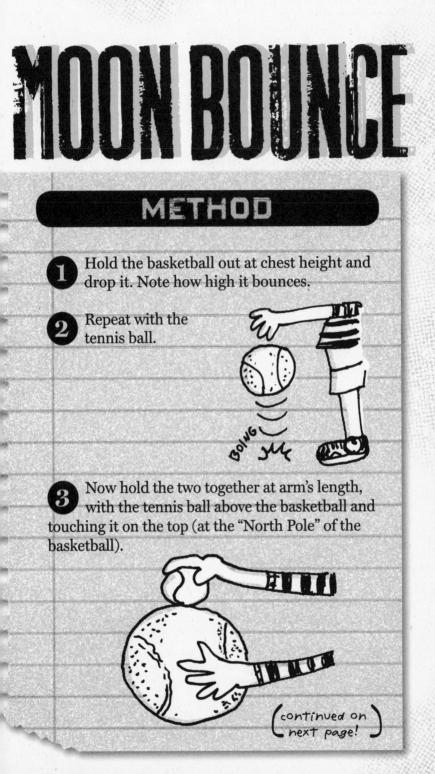

BOING

**3** Now hold the two together at arm's length, with the tennis ball above the basketball and touching it on the top (at the "North Pole" of the basketball).

(continued on next page!)

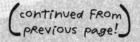
(continued from previous page!)

**4** Drop the pair together and note how high the tennis ball bounces.

**5** If it's hard to get the alignment right, try using a golf ball beneath a Ping-Pong ball.

**6** And if it's still difficult, hold the golf ball and Ping-Pong ball inside a cardboard tube (to align them with each other and vertically): This should make it easier to perform.

*TAKE CARE!* **PROVIDED YOU'VE GIVEN YOURSELF ENOUGH SPACE TO PERFORM THIS EXPERIMENT (I.E., YOU'RE OUTDOORS), THERE SHOULD BE NO CONCERNS.**

## The Scientific Excuse

This is a wonderful demonstration of conservation of momentum. Momentum can be expressed as mass × velocity. When the balls collide, their momentums are equal, but because the mass of the basketball is so much greater, the tennis ball acquires a much greater velocity to balance the equation. The result: It shoots off into space. The same principle applies to a baseball bat (massive) hitting a ball (less massive): The ball goes over the fence for a homer while the bat remains in the batter's hands.

# DANCING MOTHBALLS

IF THERE'S SUCH A THING AS JUMPING BEANS, WHY CAN'T there also be dancing mothballs? In just a few easy steps, you'll see how easy it is to make them. How in the world is all of this irresponsible? Well, just look at those ingredients and imagine how your kitchen will smell after you mix them. How popular will you be then?

## *You Will Need*

- WIDEMOUTH GLASS JAR OR DRINKING GLASS
- WATER
- 4 TABLESPOONS VINEGAR
- 2 TEASPOONS BAKING SODA
- SEVERAL MOTHBALLS

*TAKE CARE!* THIS IS A FAIRLY LOW-RISK EXPERIMENT. MAKE SURE YOU DISCARD THE LIQUID AND ITS CONTENTS AFTERWARD SO THE NEXT PERSON IN THE KITCHEN ISN'T TEMPTED TO DRINK IT!

# METHOD

**1** Fill the jar or glass with water, leaving an inch at the top.

**2** Add the vinegar and baking soda and stir gently to combine.

**3** Add 2 or 3 mothballs.

**4** Watch as the mothballs slowly "dance"—sinking first, then slowly rising, then sinking again.

## The Scientific Excuse

The vinegar, baking soda, and water react to release carbon dioxide. The mothballs seem smooth, but in fact they have very rough and uneven surfaces. Carbon dioxide bubbles can lodge on these surfaces. When enough bubbles are attached, the mothballs become less dense than the liquid and rise to the top. At the surface, much of the carbon dioxide is released into the surrounding air, making the mothballs denser once more and allowing them to sink . . . and repeat the process.

# The CD HOVERCRAFT

**IT'S EVERYONE'S DREAM TO BE ABLE TO GLIDE AROUND AS IF** they were on a flying saucer. That type of friction-free movement does, in fact, lie at the heart of hovercraft technology. This experiment lets you use everyday objects as a gateway to this brave new world of transport. Be careful, though: Get your answer straight before you hear, "What have you done to my new Kanye West CD?"

## You Will Need

- SHARP SCISSORS
- PLASTIC BOTTLE CAP
- STRONG GLUE
- ORDINARY CD OR DVD
- 7- OR 8-INCH BALLOON

*TAKE CARE!* BE CAREFUL NOT TO USE TOO MUCH GLUE WHEN ATTACHING THE CAP TO THE CD (YOU MIGHT BLOCK PART OF THE HOLE). AS MENTIONED ALREADY, DON'T USE ANYONE'S PRECIOUS NEW CD!

# METHOD

**1** Make a ½-inch hole in the center of the cap by piercing it with the scissors. Slowly rotate the scissors, widening the hole, until it is ½ inch across.

**2** Glue the flat side of the cap to the center of the CD or DVD so that the holes align, and let the glue dry.

**3** Blow up the balloon and twist the end tight (but do not tie it off).

**4** Carefully roll the balloon's "lip" over the edge of the cap.

**5** Place the CD or DVD on a smooth surface and release.

**6** The "hovercraft" should slide easily along the surface after having had the slightest touch.

zoom

## The Scientific Excuse

Air rushes out of the balloon through the hole to provide an air cushion below the CD. This cushion supports the entire lower surface of the CD because air is escaping on all sides. And without the friction of rubbing against the surface (the air cushion has eliminated it), the "hovercraft" can move freely. The same principles enable real hovercrafts to transport passengers and cars across open water.

# TWO-STAGE
# ROCKET

THE NASA WEBSITE POINTS OUT THAT rocket technology is just a variation on balloon technology, so mastering a two-stage balloon rocket should put you in the same engineering elite that produced the NASA space shuttles and the proposed Mars missions. It's wonderful to think that some of the same scientific principles are at work in this backyard demonstration anyone can master. It's not rocket science after all, or is it?

*TAKE CARE!* THIS EXPERIMENT WORKS BEST (THE STAGES TRAVEL FARTHER) IF THE FISHING LINE IS VERY TAUT AND ALSO LEVEL. THIS REDUCES FRICTION ALONG THE TRACK.

## You Will Need

- SCISSORS
- PLASTIC DRINKING STRAW
- 80–100 FEET OF CLEAR FISHING LINE
- EMPTY 1-LITER PLASTIC BOTTLE
- 2 LONG, NARROW PARTY BALLOONS (THE KIND USED TO MAKE ANIMAL FIGURES)
- MASKING TAPE

Dude, where's my rocket?

# METHOD

**1** With the scissors, cut the straw into 1-inch pieces.

**2** Thread two pieces of straw on the fishing line.

**3** Find 2 strong objects between 80 and 100 feet apart and tie the fishing line taut between them.

**4** Cut a 1 inch wide ring of plastic from the middle of the plastic bottle with the scissors. It's easier to do this if you poke a hole through the plastic first, then wedge your scissors blade through and start cutting around the bottle.

**5** Blow up one balloon and pinch it shut; press this pinched end to the inside of the plastic ring. (This balloon is the second stage of the rocket, and the next balloon will take over from your fingers to stop the first balloon from leaking air.)

**6** Continue holding the pinched mouth of the first balloon against the inside of the ring while you insert the second uninflated balloon partway through the ring so that the end of it extends a little beyond the pinched mouth of the first balloon.

**7** Now blow up the second balloon, letting go of the end of the first balloon only when it has been pressed to the inside of the ring by the inflation of the second balloon.

**8** Pinch the mouth of the second balloon: You should now have a "two-stage rocket" in your hands.

**9** Have a volunteer tape each balloon "stage" to one section of straw (which is free to slide along the fishing line). Still pinching the end of the balloon, pull the combination back to the end of the line.

**10** Initiate blastoff by letting go of the second balloon, sending the pair of them off. Once the first stage deflates, thereby releasing the pressure on the inside of the ring, the second stage (first balloon) rushes off.

### The Scientific Excuse

"For every action, there is an equal and opposite reaction." This principle, observed by Newton, lies at the heart of rocket (or in this case, balloon) science. Basically, the plastic ring serves mainly as a solid object against which the mouth of the first balloon is pressed. That pressure—holding in the air of the first balloon—is temporarily maintained by your fingers until the pressure of the soon-to-be inflated second balloon takes over. Letting go of the balloon allows the high-pressure air to rush out into the less pressurized air around it. But this rushing out provokes an opposite force, which propels the rocket forward. The same process is repeated when the first stage is depleted and it's the turn of the second stage to push ahead.

# Chapter Five

# A LOT *of* HOT AIR

**S**ome of the most amusing and magical experiments are the ones that call on an invisible ingredient—the air around us—to play a starring role. Many of the experiments in this chapter have that magical aura, putting air to work to make things float, stick, and fly. You'll have your audience eating out of the palm of your hand when they "get wind" of these experiments.

# The Hovering BALL

**HAS YOUR MOM EVER PHONED A HAIRDRESSER AND TRIED** to make an appointment for a "Bernoulli"? No? Maybe she should, because hairdressers have a tool to demonstrate one of the most far-reaching principles of physics, first noted by Daniel Bernoulli in the eighteenth century. Take 30 seconds to grasp the essence of Bernoulli's timeless observation. In the meantime, have a ball!

## You Will Need

- BLOW-DRYER
- PING-PONG BALL
- CARDBOARD PAPER TOWEL TUBE

*TAKE CARE!* THIS EXPERIMENT USES AN ELECTRICAL APPLIANCE, SO AN ADULT SHOULD SUPERVISE IT. ALWAYS REMEMBER TO KEEP ELECTRICAL APPLIANCES WELL AWAY FROM WATER. REMEMBER, IT'S THE MOVEMENT OF THE AIR—AND NOT THE HEAT—THAT MAKES THE EXPERIMENT WORK, SO USE THE COOLEST SETTING ON THE BLOW-DRYER.

# METHOD

**1** Set the blow-dryer to a low temperature but high speed and point it upward.

**2** Lower the ball into the upward flow of air and let go.

**3** Watch as the ball remains suspended.

**4** With the ball still suspended, slowly lower the cardboard tube toward it.

**5** The ball will be sucked up through the tube and out the other end.

## The Scientific Excuse

This experiment works because of Bernoulli's principle. Bernoulli, an eighteenth-century Swiss scientist, noted that a gas or liquid loses pressure as it gains speed. In this case, the air moves from the blow-dryer and around the ball, and this moving air has low pressure. The pressure remains unchanged (stronger) in the calmer air outside the column of moving air, plus in the air behind the ball. These forces keep the ball from moving too far to the left or right—or even upward. Adding the tube from above channels the moving air into the narrower space. This makes the air gain speed—and lose pressure—so the ball follows it upward.

# VIKING

**VIKING WARRIORS WHO DIED IN BATTLE WOULD BE SENT TO** Valhalla (Odin's great hall) in style: A longboat would be set ablaze and sent off to the open sea with the dearly departed in it. You can add some flourishes to the basic structure of the boat in this experiment to give it a real Viking flavor. The experiment should be performed on the calm waters of a small pond or lake.

# FUNERAL

## You Will Need

- ALUMINUM TUBE USED FOR TABLETS OR PILLS (ABOUT 4 INCHES LONG) WITH A SCREW TOP

- SMALL PIECE OF WOOD

- NAIL OR DRILL

- HAMMER

- WATER

- FOUR 1/2-INCH CANDLES, ALREADY BURNED OR CUT DOWN TO 1/2-INCH STUMPS

- AN EMPTY SHALLOW CAN (E.G., FROM SARDINES) JUST LARGE ENOUGH TO HOLD THE ALUMINUM TUBE LENGTHWISE

- MATCHES

**1** Lay the screw top of the minum tube face up on a piece of wood or something else you won't mind scratching up a bit. Hammer a nail off-center into and through the screw top. Steam will be able to escape from it later.

**2** Fill the tube halfway with water and screw the top back on.

**3** Place the candles in the can, in a line against a long side. You can secure them in position by first dripping a little wax into the can and pressing them into the melted wax.

*TAKE CARE!* ON A PRACTICAL LEVEL, NOTE THAT THE VESSEL IS QUITE FRAGILE SO IT'S BEST TO WAIT FOR CALM WEATHER AND WATER CONDITIONS BEFORE CONDUCTING THE EXPERIMENT.

**4** Place the tube (with the hole on top) lengthwise inside the can against the other long side, and secure it in the same way. The candles and tube should all fit quite snugly.

**5** Light the candles and place the can on the surface of the water.

**6** Watch as the "Viking longboat" begins to travel under its own head of steam.

### The Scientific Excuse

The candles heat the water inside the tube. This water soon boils and the steam needs to find an escape route: the small hole. The steam expands quickly and creates a noticeable recoil as it leaves the narrow opening.

Who stole my helmet?

# The Bold Little BALL

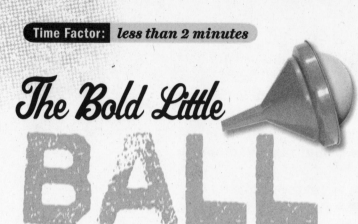

THIS EXPERIMENT IS A LITTLE GEM. IT HAS JUST TWO ingredients and can be performed in a matter of seconds. But irresponsible? Well, it's not messy, or loud, or likely to give anyone an electric shock. But it *could* become dangerous if you dare someone else to blow the ball from the funnel. Then you might need to take cover from your purple-faced—and very frustrated—friend!

## You Will Need

- PING-PONG BALL
- NARROW-MOUTHED FUNNEL (A KITCHEN FUNNEL IS IDEAL)

*TAKE CARE!* LUCKILY, THERE'S NO DIRECT RISK ASSOCIATED WITH THIS EXPERIMENT. IF YOU CHOOSE TO DARE PEOPLE TO TRY IT—OR EVEN MAKE A BET—THEN YOU MIGHT FACE SOME ANGRY REACTIONS . . .

# METHOD

 Put the ball into the funnel and hold it upright.

 Tilt your head back and put the mouth of the funnel to your lips.

**3** Blow.

**4** While blowing, slowly tilt the funnel so that it should "pour out" the ball—but notice it does not!

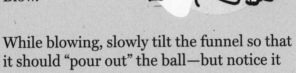

## The Scientific Excuse

Here is where things get even better. The ball stays in place because of the Bernoulli effect—the same scientific reason that a jumbo jet stays airborne. Basically, the Bernoulli effect describes how moving air (in this case, the air rushing into the funnel and along its sides) has lower pressure than air that's still. A light object, such as a feather or the ball in this experiment, will move to the area of lower pressure: The air behind the ball—even when the funnel is pointing down—has higher pressure and keeps the ball in place.

# The UNPOPPABLE

HERE'S ANOTHER ONE OF THOSE EXPERIMENTS THAT'S SO startling, so counterintuitive, that you should really perform it as a magic trick. After all, how often have you seen—much less been able to perform yourself—a demonstration as baffling as this one? And if that weren't enough of a billing, it's really easy to do.

# BALLOON

## *You Will Need*

- BALLOON (ANY SIZE WILL DO)
- 12-INCH COOKING SKEWER
- COOKING OIL

# METHOD

**1** Inflate the balloon, almost but not quite fully. Tie it off as you would normally.

**2** Coat the skewer on both sides with cooking oil.

**3** Hold the skewer with one hand and the balloon in the other (making sure that the knot of the balloon is on the balloon's "equator" rather than on one of the "poles"). If you're doing it as a trick, you could have an assistant hold the balloon.

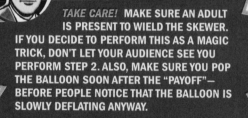

*TAKE CARE!* MAKE SURE AN ADULT IS PRESENT TO WIELD THE SKEWER. IF YOU DECIDE TO PERFORM THIS AS A MAGIC TRICK, DON'T LET YOUR AUDIENCE SEE YOU PERFORM STEP 2. ALSO, MAKE SURE YOU POP THE BALLOON SOON AFTER THE "PAYOFF"— BEFORE PEOPLE NOTICE THAT THE BALLOON IS SLOWLY DEFLATING ANYWAY.

**4** Slowly pierce the balloon with the skewer, twisting slowly and taking care to enter at the knot and to exit exactly opposite (where there should still be a small amount of slack).

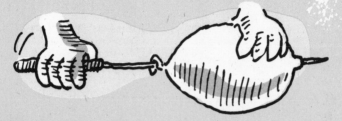

**5** Equally carefully, remove the skewer; hold the balloon by pinching the far hole. The balloon still will not burst although you will notice it slowly losing air.

**6** Puncture the balloon deliberately by quickly piercing the stretched side of the balloon.

## The Scientific Excuse

The rubber of the balloon consists of many interlinked long molecules, known as polymers. The molecules are held together in a pattern called cross-linking, which allows for some elasticity. If there's still some slack in the cross-linking (as there is in the knotted end and its opposite extreme), the polymers can "close ranks" around a small incision. The rubber actually forms a seal around the skewer that has just pierced it. Lubricating the skewer makes this entrance a little easier, and it helps provide a temporary patch when the skewer is removed. At the end of the experiment, you can burst the balloon easily by puncturing the stretched side, which hasn't enough slack to form a protective seal.

# The Clinking
# COLA

"MOM, COULD I FINISH OFF that bottle of cola so I can learn more about air pressure?" "Yes—unless burping is what you mean by air pressure!"

## You Will Need

- EMPTY GLASS COLA BOTTLE (OR ANY GLASS BOTTLE)
- QUARTER

*TAKE CARE!* THE ONLY RISK YOU'LL RUN WITH THIS EXPERIMENT IS THE TOUCH OF INDIGESTION YOU MAY GET IF YOU DOWN THE ENTIRE BOTTLE OF COLA IN ONE LONG GULP IN ORDER TO EMPTY IT.

# METHOD

**1** Keep the cola bottle somewhere cool for a few hours or preferably overnight (you could even scour an outdoor recycling bin for a cool one!).

**2** Bring the cooled glass bottle indoors, moisten the rim, and put the coin on its open mouth.

**3** Wrap your hands around the bottle.

**4** Wait until the coin begins to move as if being fingered by an unseen hand.

## The Scientific Excuse

The air inside the cooled bottle takes up relatively little space, but as it warms up (because of your hands) it tries to expand. This would-be expansion builds up pressure inside the bottle, but water tension holds the coin in place. Eventually, the pressure is enough to overcome the water tension—briefly—allowing some of the air to escape. The coin pops open when this happens, then settles again when the air pressure inside has dropped again.

**MATCH ALERT!**
This experiment involves the use of matches and should be conducted only with a responsible adult present

# *Tea Bag*
# HOT-AIR
# BALLOON

THERE'S SOMETHING MAGICAL ABOUT TAKING AN EVERYDAY object and getting it to behave in a particularly unpredictable way. In this case, the object is a humble tea bag, which can be carefully taken apart and then set alight. The tea bag will float upward, as if by magic. Because even a slight puff of wind could disrupt this delicate experiment, it's best done inside—or outdoors in very sheltered surroundings on a calm day.

## *You Will Need*

- **TEA BAG (THE SORT WITH A STRING AND TAG)**
- **STAPLE REMOVER (OR STRONG FINGERNAILS)**
- **SMALL PLATE**
- **MATCHES**

# METHOD

**1** Remove the string from the tea bag.

**2** Use a staple remover or your fingernails to remove the staple from the tea bag.

**3** Unfold the tea bag and pour the loose tea out of it.

**4** Stand the emptied tea bag—which is now shaped like a cylinder—on its end on a small plate.

**5** Light a match and set fire to the top of the tea bag.

**6** As the flame burns down, the burning tea bag will shake a little and then float up into the air.

## The Scientific Excuse

It's the old story—"hot air rises"—at work here. The fire causes two things to happen. One is that the air around the tea bag gets hotter and hotter. Another is that—because of the burning—the tea bag loses weight (or mass, if you want to be really scientific). These two factors converge, eventually reaching a point where the air is warm enough—and the tea bag light enough—to produce liftoff.

# *The* LAST

SOME OF THE BEST SCIENCE EXPERIMENTS ARE THE ONES that overturn our preconceptions, prompting calls of "That's not right—it can't be." This experiment is a fine example of one of those myth busters, bound to get someone hot under the collar. Drinking through a straw is a piece of cake, isn't it? Well, maybe not always. . . .

## *You Will Need*

- CLEAN GLASS OR PLASTIC JAR WITH TIGHT-FITTING LID (AN EMPTY JELLY JAR WORKS WELL)

- PLASTIC DRINKING STRAW

- HAMMER AND NAIL

- SCREWDRIVER

- MODELING CLAY

- WATER

STRAW!

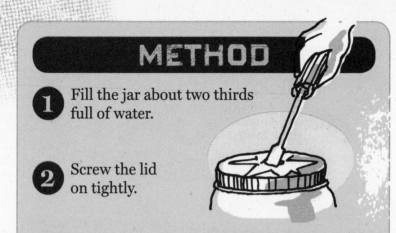

1. Fill the jar about two thirds full of water.

2. Screw the lid on tightly.

3. Use the hammer and nail to make a hole in the lid; use the screwdriver to work the hole until it's wide enough for the straw to fit through it.

4. Slide the straw down through the lid, judging how far down it should go by lining the lid up against the jar.

5. Seal the edge of the hole around the straw with some modeling clay, working it in so there's no gap at all.

6. Screw the lid back on the jar and try to drink through the straw. You—or your disgruntled volunteer—should find it impossible.

## The Scientific Excuse

The preconception here is that we suck water directly when we drink through a straw. This experiment shows that it's all about air and air pressure. The air around us exerts pressure on everything it touches, including the surface of a drink in a glass or open jar. When you put a straw in a drink normally (that is, when the drink is in an uncovered container), the pressure of the air on the drink is the same as the pressure of the air coming through the straw. But when you suck on the straw, you remove some of the air and reduce the pressure in the air that's left in the straw. The air pressing down on the surface of the drink, however, still has the same pressure. The difference in pressure pushes the liquid into—and through—the straw. Sealing the lid tightly blocks the outside air from pressing down on the liquid in the jar, so now matter how much you suck, there's no pressure from inside to force the liquid into the straw.

# BALLOON POWER

WE OFTEN LOSE SIGHT OF THE FACT THAT AIR HAS MASS and exerts pressure. Sure, we all hear weather forecasters talking about air pressure, but that's a little abstract. This experiment brings it all home, though, and is something of a work in progress. Some children have managed to attach more than two dozen cups to their balloons: See how (and why that amount is so impressive) by reading on.

## You Will Need

- STRONG BALLOON
  (TEARDROP SHAPE WORKS BEST)
- 6 PLASTIC CUPS
  (OR TRY MORE IF YOU SUCCEED WITH THE EXPERIMENT)

*TAKE CARE!* SOME PEOPLE OBVIOUSLY HAVE A KNACK FOR SUCCEEDING WITH THIS EXPERIMENT, BUT EVEN THE LEAST EXPERIENCED EXPERIMENTER SHOULD BE ABLE TO GET AT LEAST TWO CUPS TO STICK. MAKE SURE YOU KEEP A LITTLE PRESSURE ON EACH CUP JUST AFTER ATTACHING IT SO THAT IT WILL "TAKE."

# METHOD

 **1** Blow up the balloon until it's about the size of a grapefruit. Pinch it shut temporarily.

 **2** Wet the rims of 2 plastic cups.

 **3** Press the rims of the cups against the sides balloon and continue to inflate the balloon. The cups should stay attached to the balloon.

**4** Repeat the process—pinch, wet, press, and inflate—seeing how many cups you can attach to one balloon.

## The Scientific Excuse

As mentioned in the introduction, this experiment is all about air pressure and its counterpart, suction. Wetting the rims of the cups allows them to stick on initially because of water tension. But by inflating the balloon—and reducing the curvature of balloon coming in contact with the rims—the air pressure inside the cups reduces somewhat because the same amount of air now fills more space. The air pressure outside the cups, however, remains the same. This difference of pressure causes the cups to be pushed into the balloon.

# Chapter Six

# 100% NATURAL

**M**other Nature is conducting all sorts of experiments—irresponsible or otherwise—all around us all the time. The following chapter takes the lid off some of her secrets and leaves the lid firmly shut on those that need darkness and time in order to work out. Flex your scientific muscles a little and then try your hand at directing plants, creating blubber, or turning brittle bones to rubber. How can you do all this? Just act "naturally" and read on.

# Pond-Life
# PALS

**BRINGING SMELLY, SLIMY WATER WEEDS INTO THE FRESHLY** cleaned kitchen? Erm, it's "all in the cause of science": This experiment helps us learn that plants really are the "lungs" of the world around us.

**MATCH ALERT!**
This experiment involves the use of matches and should be conducted only with a responsible adult present.

## You Will Need

- 2-PINT WIDEMOUTH GLASS JAR
- WATER
- 3–4 WATERWEED SHOOTS FROM A GARDEN POND OR LAKE
- 3 CLOTHESPINS
- SMALL FUNNEL (TO FIT EASILY WITHIN JAR)
- 3-INCH LONG TEST TUBE
- MATCHES

*TAKE CARE!* MAKE SURE THAT YOU HAVEN'T KILLED YOUR OXYGEN PRODUCERS ON THE WAY FROM THE GARDEN POND (SEE STEP 2). BE PATIENT SO THAT ENOUGH OXYGEN BUILDS UP. BE CAREFUL WHEN HANDLING MATCHES BUT AT THE SAME TIME REMEMBER THAT THE MATCH HEAD STILL NEEDS TO BE GLOWING SOMEWHAT IF THE OXYGEN IS TO DO ITS PARTY TRICK.

# METHOD

**1** Fill the jar with fresh water and add the waterweed.

**2** Make sure that your waterweed specimens are still alive by checking to see that they emit bubbles once underwater.

**3** Clip the clothespins to the wide rim of the funnel to form a tripod.

**4** Lower the funnel tripod down so that most of the shoots are inside the cone. Make sure the narrow end of the funnel is higher than the water level.

**5** Place the test tube over this end of the funnel.

**6** Wait for 2 hours and then remove the test tube carefully, keeping it upside down.

**7** Have someone light a match and then blow it out.

**8** With the match head still glowing, drop it inside the test tube. Make sure to face the test tube away from you or anyone around you. The match will ignite.

## The Scientific Excuse

The bubbles coming up from the plants and trapped by the test tube are oxygen, a by-product of the food-producing process called photosynthesis. After an hour or two, enough oxygen has been collected to provide the fuel for the combustion of the glowing match.

# *The* RUBBER *Chicken* BONE

HAVE YOU EVER STRUGGLED WITH A DRUMSTICK WHEN they've served chicken at school? You take a bite and chew . . . and chew . . . and chew. After you've finally managed to swallow it you feel the need to come up for air before trying another bite. You need stamina for this sort of meal, after all. That's when you begin to wonder whether you've been eating a rubber chicken rather than a real one. Then you think, "That's ridiculous! Who ever heard of a rubber chicken?" Try this experiment and you might begin to think otherwise.

## *You Will Need*

- **GOOD-SIZED CHICKEN THIGH OR DRUMSTICK, LEFT OVER FROM A MEAL**
- **LIDDED JAR BIG ENOUGH TO HOLD THE BONE WITH SOME ROOM TO SPARE**
- **VINEGAR**

*TAKE CARE!* THIS EXPERIMENT IS SAFE AND YOU RUN ONLY A RISK IF YOU SPILL THE VINEGAR-CHICKEN BONE MIXTURE. MAKE SURE IT'S NOWHERE NEAR CARPETS OR EXPENSIVE FURNITURE.

# METHOD

1. Thoroughly clean the meat from the bone.

2. Rinse the bone under running water.

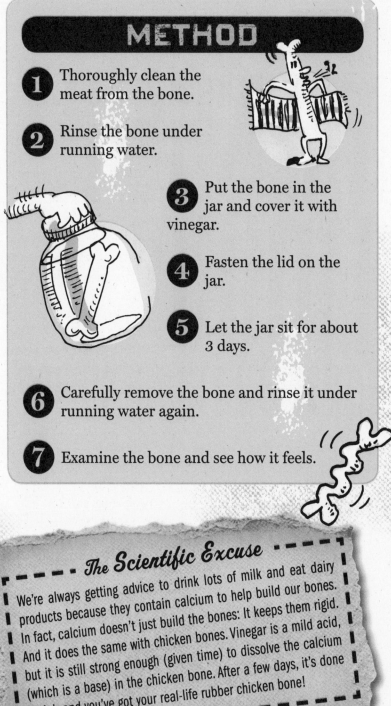

3. Put the bone in the jar and cover it with vinegar.

4. Fasten the lid on the jar.

5. Let the jar sit for about 3 days.

6. Carefully remove the bone and rinse it under running water again.

7. Examine the bone and see how it feels.

## The Scientific Excuse

We're always getting advice to drink lots of milk and eat dairy products because they contain calcium to help build our bones. In fact, calcium doesn't just build the bones: It keeps them rigid. And it does the same with chicken bones. Vinegar is a mild acid, but it is still strong enough (given time) to dissolve the calcium (which is a base) in the chicken bone. After a few days, it's done its job and you've got your real-life rubber chicken bone!

# THE SOLID LIQUID
## [OR IS IT A LIQUID SOLID?]

**WE ALL KNOW THAT LIQUIDS WILL TURN TO** solids when it's cold enough and that solids (like ice) will melt when things warm up. But how can you explain something that goes from liquid to solid when you tap it, then decides to be a liquid again when you treat it gently? Find out below.

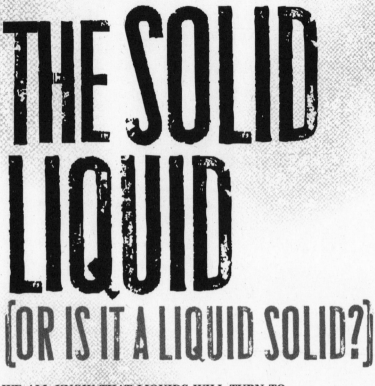

*TAKE CARE!* THERE ARE NO REAL RISKS HERE, APART FROM THOSE ASSOCIATED WITH MAKING A MESS ON THE KITCHEN TABLE.

# You Will Need

- 1 CUP CORNSTARCH
- LARGE MIXING BOWL
- FOOD COLORING
- ½ CUP WATER

**1** Add the cornstarch to the bowl and mix in a few drops of food coloring.

**2** Slowly add the water to the bowl and, using your fingers, mix it with the cornstarch. Don't necessarily use all the water: Stop when all the powder is wet.

**3** Continue mixing with your fingers and then tap the surface of the mixture. If the surface feels solid even though the mixture just felt like a liquid when you were mixing, then you've got it right.

**4** If the mixture is too powdery, add some more water; if it's too liquid, add some more cornstarch.

**5** Try different ways of handling the mixture—rolling it into a ball and then holding it in your palm, banging it with a mixing spoon, flattening it—to see how it behaves.

**6** Ask others to decide what its natural state is: solid or liquid?

Help me!
I'm sinking!

# SELF-SEAL SANDWICH BAG

IT'S GREAT THAT A SANDWICH BAG CAN KEEP YOUR LUNCH fresh for hours, but isn't it a hassle having to pinch the top, get rid of the excess air, and then pull the zip *all the way across*? Surely there must be some way of saving us all that effort. Could this experiment be a step in that direction? Let's hope so—we might see an end to the condition of chronic "sandwich bag-tug" fatigue.

## You Will Need

- ZIPLOCK SANDWICH BAG
- WATER
- 3 SHARP PENCILS

*TAKE CARE!* IT'S BEST TO DO THIS EXPERIMENT EITHER OUTDOORS OR OVER A SINK OR BOWL—THE PENCIL REMOVAL CAN GET A LITTLE MESSY IF YOU'RE NOT CAREFUL. IF YOU'RE FEELING ECOLOGICALLY SOUND, YOU COULD BE LESS WASTEFUL BY USING A SANDWICH BAG THAT YOU'VE BROUGHT HOME FROM SCHOOL (HAVING USED IT AT LUNCH THAT DAY).

# METHOD

 **1** Fill the sandwich bag about two thirds of the way with water.

 **2** Seal the bag as you would normally.

 **3** Holding the top of the bag, pierce the side with a pencil below the water level and continue until it emerges from the far side of the bag.

 **4** Repeat Step 3 with the second and third pencils.

**5** Note how the sandwich bag seals each hole—at least while the pencil is inside!

## The Scientific Excuse

Rather like the rubber in the Unpoppable Balloon (page 122), the plastic in many sandwich bags is naturally elastic—up to a point. Having been punctured by a sharp object, the plastic will form a seal around the edge of the hole. Unfortunately, this power doesn't quite extend to plugging the hole again when the pencil is removed, so be forewarned.

# ROSES ARE RED?

**CLEVER FLORISTS MANAGE TO GET GREEN CARNATIONS FOR** St. Patrick's Day each year. Did you ever wonder how? Here's your chance to get in on the secret.

## You Will Need

- 2 FOUNTAIN PEN INK CARTRIDGES (1 RED AND 1 GREEN)
- 2 TEST TUBES
- WATER
- SHARP KNIFE
- WHITE-BLOSSOM FLOWER (E.G., ROSE OR CARNATION) WITH A 6- TO 8-INCH STEM
- 10-OUNCE DRINKING GLASS

*TAKE CARE!* MAKE SURE THE SPLIT PART OF THE STEM IS MAINLY SUBMERGED SINCE IT COULD ALLOW TOO MUCH AIR IN OTHERWISE, KILLING THE PLANT AND RUINING YOUR EXPERIMENT.

# METHOD

 **1** Pour each ink cartridge into a separate test tube.

 **2** Dilute the ink by half-filling each tube with water.

**3** With a knife, carefully slit the stem of the flower so that its base has 2 halves, each as long as a test tube. The stem should remain whole above the slit.

**4** Put one stem half in each test tube and place the tubes (still holding the stem) inside the glass.

 **5** Keep the tubes upright for several hours.

**6** The blossom will have changed color gradually—one part becoming red and the other part turning green.

## The Scientific Excuse

The diluted ink is mainly water, which the plant needs for nourishment. It travels through the narrow channels that transport water and nutrients to the different parts of a plant. The coloring (in reality, tiny particles of solid) hits the end of the line when it reaches the blossom, although the accompanying water either is used by the plant or evaporates from the surface of the blossom. What remains is the distinct color.

# The RUNAWAY PLANT

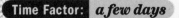

**THIS WONDERFUL "STAND BACK AND WATCH" EXPERIMENT** highlights one of the most basic—and at the same time amazing—properties of plants. Just like that seedling that pokes its way through asphalt, the growing potato will work its way through the maze you've built just to find the nearest source of light. If only we were all so resourceful and persistent!

## You Will Need

- RULER
- SHOEBOX
- SCISSORS
- 2-FOOT X 2-FOOT STIFF CARDBOARD
- SPROUTING POTATO
- MOIST SOIL
- SMALL FLOWERPOT (SHORTER THAN THE HEIGHT OF THE SHOEBOX)

FEED ME!

**1** Measure the inside dimensions (height and width) of the shoebox and cut 3 shapes of cardboard to that size. These will act as partitions inside the shoebox.

**2** Cover the potato with moist soil in the flowerpot.

**3** Check that each card shape fits snugly in the shoebox as a vertical barrier.

**4** Cut a hole in each partition just wider than the diameter of the potato sprout. Each hole should be in a different position on the cardboard from the others.

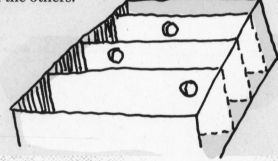

*TAKE CARE!* **THIS IS A SAFE EXPERIMENT AND HOLDS NO CONCERNS FOR THOSE CONDUCTING IT. THEN AGAIN, IF YOU WERE TO TRY SEALING THE POTATO INSIDE YOUR DAD'S SHOE INSTEAD OF A SHOEBOX—SAY, A FAVORITE PAIR OF RUNNING SNEAKERS—THEN THIS EXPERIMENT CAN BE SAID TO BE TRULY IRRESPONSIBLE (UNLESS YOUR DAD DOESN'T MIND HAVING THINGS SPROUT FROM THE SHOELACE HOLES!).**

**5** Cut a fourth hole on the upright end of the shoebox.

**6** Slide the partitions into the shoebox, regularly spaced apart. Put the flowerpot in the shoebox at the end farthest from the end with the hole in it.

**7** Replace the lid carefully on the shoebox, making sure no light can get into it. Put the shoebox on a surface where light will shine through the top.

**8** Leave the box and after a few days you will see the shoot edging through the hole in the top end of the box.

**9** Open the lid to see the path the shoot took to get there.

## The Scientific Excuse

You've just demonstrated a principle called tropism, which explains how a plant reacts to an outside stimulus. Tropism can take different forms: The roots of a plant going down—or out—to find water demonstrates one sort. This experiment demonstrates another, called heliotropism, which describes a plant's efforts to find light.

# *Sunny* EXPOSURE

**JUST WHY IS IT THAT PLANTS SEEM TO NEED SO MUCH LIGHT?** Can they get by without it and still look their best? Well, we're not going to tell you. But we've got a way of letting you find out for yourself, provided you're patient enough to wait a week.

## *You Will Need*

- SCISSORS
- SEVERAL SHEETS OF BLACK CONSTRUCTION PAPER
- HEALTHY, GOOD-SIZED GERANIUM PLANT
- MASKING TAPE

It's getting hot in here...

**TAKE CARE!** BE GENTLE WHEN ATTACHING THE PAPER TO AND REMOVING IT FROM THE LEAVES, WHICH ARE DELICATE. A HEART IS A DELICATE SHAPE, TOO: SO SWEET! BUT IF YOU WANT TO BE A LITTLE LESS SWEET, PERHAPS A BIT MORE IRRESPONSIBLE, THINK OF SOME OTHER SHAPE OR MESSAGE YOU WOULD LIKE TO SEE STENCILED ON THE PAPER: NOTHING YOU WOULDN'T WANT SOMEONE ELSE TO READ, RIGHT?

Cut 2 squares of construction paper so that each is slightly larger than the geranium leaf.

 Draw a heart shape in the middle of one of these squares and cut it out carefully, leaving the border of the square intact.

 Choose a leaf on the plant and carefully sandwich it between the squares of paper, placing the square with the cutout heart on the top. Secure the borders of the squares together with tape.

 Repeat this process with 2 or 3 more leaves.

Wait for a week.

 Carefully remove the papers from the leaves. You should see a lovely green heart surrounded by pale leaf tissue.

## The Scientific Excuse

The green that we associate with plants (and find in healthy geranium leaves) comes from a chemical called chlorophyll. This chemical is produced in the chemical process known as photosynthesis (the way that plants produce their own food, using light as an ingredient). This experiment exposes only part of the leaves to the light—which explains the bright green hearts once you remove the papers. The areas that were covered have changed to pale green, yellow, or—in extreme cases—white.

# DO-IT-YOURSELF
## BLUBBER

**POLAR BEARS, WHALES, AND SEALS CAN LIVE MOST OF THEIR** lives in subfreezing air or near-freezing waters, yet each of these species is a mammal. And mammals are warm-blooded creatures who need to create and preserve heat in order to survive. Here's a chance to experience the secret of these Arctic survivors. This secret is called blubber.

## *You Will Need*

- 1 CUP VEGETABLE OIL
- 4 ZIPLOCK SANDWICH BAGS
- MASKING TAPE
- SINK OR DEEP BUCKET
- COLD WATER AND ICE CUBES
- TIMER (OR WATCH WITH A SECOND HAND)

# METHOD

 Add the vegetable oil to an open sandwich bag.

 Turn a second sandwich bag inside out and insert it in the first bag.

 Zip the inside bag to the outside bag so that the cooking oil is between them.

 Tape shut any gaps where the bags join.

 Connect the other 2 sandwich bags together in the same way, only without any oil. (Each pair of bags becomes a "mitten.")

 Fill the sink or bucket with cold water and add some ice cubes to lower the temperature further.

 Put a mitten on each hand, start the timer, and submerge the mittens in the cold water.

8 Time how long you can keep each mitten— "blubber" and normal—in the water before you have to pull it out because your hand is too cold.

## The Scientific Excuse

The key to survival in very cold temperatures is preserving body heat. Blubber, the thick layer of fat under the skin of whales and seals, does that by insulating the body. In effect, it blocks the flow of heat from the body to the outside. In this experiment, the oil (petroleum jelly would work as well if you had enough of it) insulates your hand in the same way.

# Chapter Seven

# MAD SCIENCE

**T**he following pages contain some real show-stoppers—experiments that might give you the aura of a Transylvanian scientist with his sidekick, Igor. Even using everyday objects such as balloons, paper towels, coins, or playing cards, you'll be able to generate gasps from your audience. But don't forget: Your bag of tricks comes labeled "scientific principles." And the key players behind the scenes are electrical currents, air pressure, chemical reactions, and molecular movement.

# MY CUP OVERFLOWETH?

**SOMETIMES PEOPLE NEED A DEMONSTRATION THAT WILL** show them that the same hard-to-master principles of chemistry can be downright entertaining—or mystifying. See if you can work out why the cup doesn't overflow before you read the scientific excuse. For the best effect, make sure that a member of the "audience" spoons out the sugar: That way, they won't suspect you of trickery.

## You Will Need

- LARGE PITCHER
- PIPING-HOT TAP WATER
- LARGE DRINKING GLASS
- TEASPOON
- CONFECTIONERS' SUGAR

*TAKE CARE!* IF THE SURFACE TENSION OF THE WATER IS RUPTURED, THE WATER IS MORE LIKELY TO SPILL.

# METHOD

 **1** Set the glass on a table and run the faucet until the water is hot.

**2** Fill the pitcher with hot water, and then pour water from the pitcher into the glass; slow the flow as you near the top so you can get it completely full.

**3** Very carefully (with the slowest flow possible) continue to add the hot water from the pitcher until the surface of the drinking glass bulges over the top but doesn't spill.

**4** Now measure 1 teaspoon of sugar and add it to the water from just above the water surface. Make sure to do this without causing a splash or breaking the surface of the water with the teaspoon. The water shouldn't overflow despite the addition of the sugar.

**5** Repeat this process until the water does eventually overflow.

## The Scientific Excuse

We sometimes forget that there are spaces between the molecules that make up some of the most familiar substances, such as water. In this experiment, the sugar goes into solution with the water and its molecules slip into these gaps between the water molecules. So, although the glass is "full" (in fact, more than full because of water tension), it still has room for some sugar.

# The BOTTOMLESS

**YOU KNOW THOSE PEANUT-SHAPED PIECES OF STYROFOAM** that surround delicate objects sent in the mail—and seem to get everywhere? You can put these to work in a delightful experiment that cries out for an audience. There's also a good scientific explanation, so you can feel happy on that score. Just gather up those bits of Styrofoam—you'll need more of them than you'd ever imagine!

## You Will Need

- RUBBER GLOVES
- NAIL POLISH REMOVER (HANDLE WITH EXTREME CARE!)
- EMPTY SOUP CAN, RINSED WELL
- STYROFOAM PACKING PIECES (LOTS: A PILE AT LEAST AS LARGE AS A BASKETBALL)

# PIT

**TAKE CARE!** NAIL POLISH REMOVER IS SAFER THAN STRAIGHT ACETONE (ITS ACTIVE INGREDIENT), BUT REMEMBER THAT IT'S A SOLVENT AND AN IRRITANT. WEAR GLOVES WHEN DOING THIS EXPERIMENT, EVEN IF YOU MAKE THEM SEEM LIKE PART OF A MAGICIAN'S OUTFIT! AFTER PERFORMING THE EXPERIMENT, LEAVE THE CAN OUTDOORS IN A SAFE PLACE FOR A DAY OR SO. THE LIQUID WILL SOLIDIFY AND CAN BE DISPOSED OF EASILY.

# METHOD

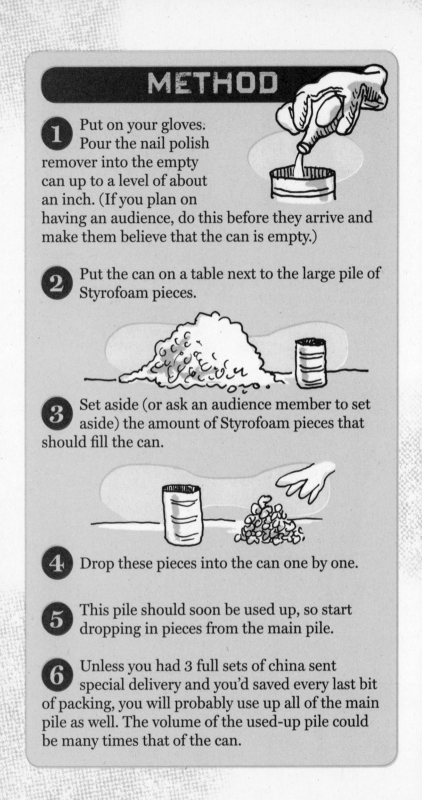

**1** Put on your gloves. Pour the nail polish remover into the empty can up to a level of about an inch. (If you plan on having an audience, do this before they arrive and make them believe that the can is empty.)

**2** Put the can on a table next to the large pile of Styrofoam pieces.

**3** Set aside (or ask an audience member to set aside) the amount of Styrofoam pieces that should fill the can.

**4** Drop these pieces into the can one by one.

**5** This pile should soon be used up, so start dropping in pieces from the main pile.

**6** Unless you had 3 full sets of china sent special delivery and you'd saved every last bit of packing, you will probably use up all of the main pile as well. The volume of the used-up pile could be many times that of the can.

## The Scientific Excuse

This experiment relies on the chemical interaction between Styrofoam and acetone, the active ingredient in nail polish remover. Styrofoam is made up of a long chain of chemical "sub-units." This chain is called a polymer ("poly" is the Greek word for *many*). The acetone dissolves the linking units of this chain. With these links gone (liquefied), there's very little left of the Styrofoam apart from air.

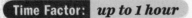

# MATCHBOX MICROPHONE

WELL, IF ACTIVISTS CAN MAKE SOAPBOX SPEECHES, WHY can't you use a much smaller box—a matchbox—to get your message across? This experiment gives you not only the chance to tinker for a good cause, but also a glimpse into the bustling world of those nineteenth-century inventors.

## You Will Need

- SAFETY PIN (FOR PIERCING THE MATCHBOX)
- BASE OF A SMALL MATCHBOX
- GRAPHITE "LEADS" FROM A MECHANICAL PENCIL
- KNIFE
- OLD PAIR OF EARPHONES OR HEADPHONES THAT YOU WON'T NEED AGAIN—IDEALLY, WITH A GOOD LENGTH OF CORD ATTACHED
- 4.5-VOLT BATTERY
- 10 INCHES CONNECTING WIRE

You light up my life . . .

TAKE CARE! MAKE SURE YOU CAN PART WITH THE HEADPHONES OR EARPHONES, SINCE IT'S MUCH HARDER TO REINSTATE THEM THAN TO TAKE THEM APART (AND THERE'S NOT MUCH LONG-TERM CALL FOR MATCHBOX COMMUNICATIONS IN THE MODERN WORLD). NOTHING ESPECIALLY IRRESPONSIBLE IN THIS ONE, UNLESS YOU DIDN'T ASK YOUR PARENTAL UNITS' PERMISSION TO DESTROY THEIR HEADPHONES.

# METHOD

**1** Pierce 2 holes, about ½ inch apart, on each of the short sides of the matchbox base. Make sure the holes line up at opposite ends.

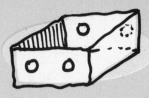

**2** Break off 3 lengths of lead. Two of these should be about ⅝ inch longer than the length of the matchbox, and the third should be ¾ inch long.

**3** Using a knife, carefully scrape some of the surface off one side of each piece of "lead."

**4** Insert the 2 long leads, scraped side up, through the sets of holes in the matchbox and lay the short length scraped side down across them.

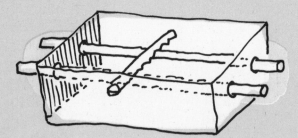

**5** Starting at the end of the earphone cord, separate the 2 strands for about 6 inches.

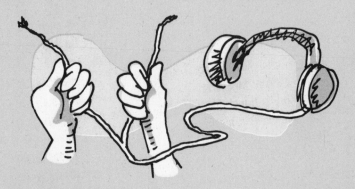

**6** Connect one strand to one of the battery flaps and the second strand to a protruding pencil lead.

**7** Use the connecting wire to connect the other pencil lead and the second battery flap, thereby completing a series circuit.

**8** Have someone else hold the earphones; pick up the matchbox carefully, holding it horizontal all the time.

**9** Speak into the matchbox—and your partner should hear your voice through the earphones.

### The Scientific Excuse

This experiment calls on the basic principle of all microphones. When you speak into the box, it vibrates because sound travels in waves, just like the ripples caused when you toss a stone into a calm pond or lake. The wave movement of the air causes the box to vibrate at just the same rhythm as the vibrations that your voice created. This movement is passed on to the leads, which cause the current to flow unevenly. The reverse happens in the earphones: The stop-start in the current causes vibrations, which are translated back to sound.

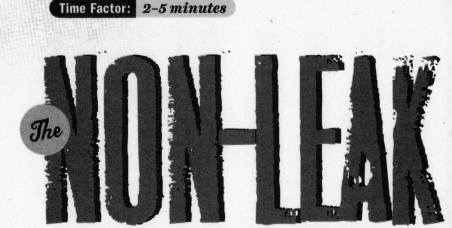

# The NON-LEAK

IS THIS AN EXPERIMENT OR IS IT REALLY A TRICK? WELL, IT works well as either—or both. Sure, it's a neat demonstration of how a couple of basic physical forces can team up in novel ways. But it's also a great way to let the family know-it-alls get what's coming to them. Anyway, there's an obvious retort to anyone who complains about it: "Don't be such a drip."

## You Will Need

- PERMANENT MARKER
- EMPTY CLEAR PLASTIC 1-LITER BOTTLE WITH SCREW CAP
- THUMBTACK
- SINK OR PAN LARGE ENOUGH TO HOLD THE BOTTLE
- WATER

*TAKE CARE!* THE TRICK HERE IS TO NOT LET THE BOTTLE LEAK TOO SOON. KEEPING THE WATER RUNNING AS YOU FILL IT ENSURES THAT THERE'S NO AIR AT THE TOP. HOLDING THE BOTTLE BY THE CAP AS YOU MOVE IT MEANS THAT IT WON'T GET SQUEEZED—ANOTHER WAY OF PRODUCING A FALSE START.

LEAK

# METHOD

**1** Use the permanent marker to write a prominent warning such as "DO NOT OPEN" on the bottle about a third of the way up.

**2** Use the thumbtack to poke a series of tiny holes in the bottle at the base of the handwritten letters.

**3** Place the bottle in a sink or pan.

**4** Fill the bottle with water and, if possible, keep the water running as you carefully tighten the screw top.

**5** Holding the bottle by the cap, place it carefully on a kitchen counter, with the handwritten warning facing out.

**6** Be patient and wait for someone to come along. Plead ignorance if they ask about the warning and watch as they become curious and open it.

**7** When the person opens the bottle, water will gush out at them from the series of tiny holes you made with the thumbtack.

## The Scientific Excuse

Everything in this experiment depends on gravity and air pressure. The two need to work in tandem to cause the water to flow out of the bottom of the bottle. When the bottle has been filled, without even the slightest amount of air at the top, gravity is unable to force the water downward because it needs the air—and air pressure—to act as an intermediary. The same force (air pressure) is holding the water back from flowing through the pinholes. When the cap is removed, gravity combines with air pressure at the top of the bottle to overcome the inward air-pressure force at the holes. The result is a sudden spouting of water on the hapless person who disregarded the warning.

# The SHOCKING TRUTH

**IT'S A TREAT WHEN A HARMLESS EVERYDAY OBJECT—IN THIS** case, a sweater—can have the starring role in a demonstration of an eye-popping scientific principle. So find yourself a cozy sweater and let those sparks fly!

## You Will Need

- WOOL SWEATER (THE THICKER THE BETTER)
- CARPETED FLOOR

*TAKE CARE!* **THERE'S ABSOLUTELY NO RISK FROM THE SMALL AMOUNT OF ELECTRICITY INVOLVED IN THIS EXPERIMENT.**

# METHOD

 **1** Perform this experiment at night or with the curtains drawn.

**2** Close the door of the room and turn off the lights.

**3** Slowly rub the sweater along the carpet.

**4** Watch as sparks fly!

## The Scientific Excuse

Our old friend static electricity is at work here. The contact of the sweater's wool against the carpet (both materials being insulators, with electrons on their surface) means that electrons can pass from one to the other. This has nothing to do with friction. Instead, the rubbing exposes more of the surfaces (wool and carpet) to each other, allowing more and more electrons to "jump ship." A chain reaction sets in, creating more heat until—snap—sparks fly.

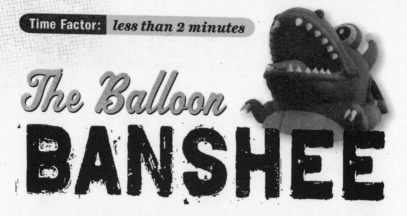

# *The Balloon* BANSHEE

**THIS DEVILISH EXPERIMENT IS SO EASY THAT YOU COULD** start it off—unnoticed—at someone's birthday party. Who could imagine that a colorful party balloon could be so . . . spooky! It's the kind of trick that gets little kids going if you do it just right. Is that irresponsible? Well, if you get a dozen 5-year-olds running from a room because they think they're hearing ghosts, one of their parents might just call you a tad irresponsible. Then again, if you explain the scientific excuse after you've scared the hee-bie-jeebies out of them, those same parents might just call you the next Einstein!

## You Will Need

- HEXAGONAL NUT (ABOUT ³/₈ TO ¹/₂ INCH ACROSS AND WITH NO SHARP EDGES)
- STRONG BALLOON

*TAKE CARE!* THIS IS A QUICK, LOW-RISK EXPERIMENT. JUST MAKE SURE YOUR NUT DOESN'T HAVE ANY SHARP OR ROUGH EDGES, WHICH COULD BURST THE BALLOON BEFORE YOU HEAR A THING.

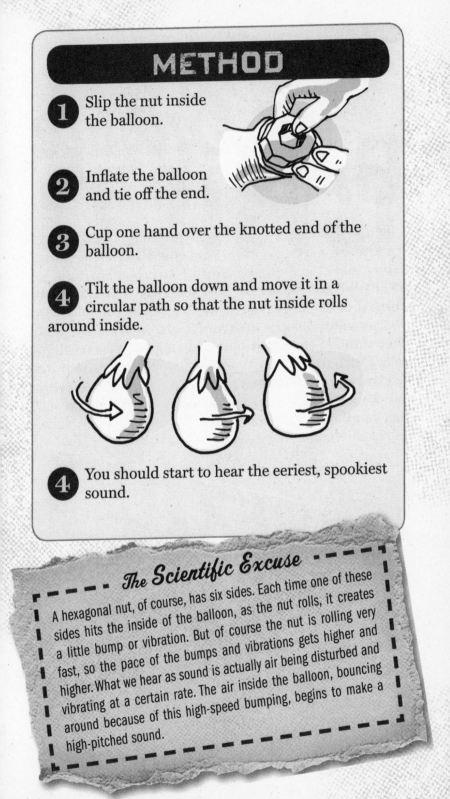

# METHOD

**1** Slip the nut inside the balloon.

**2** Inflate the balloon and tie off the end.

**3** Cup one hand over the knotted end of the balloon.

**4** Tilt the balloon down and move it in a circular path so that the nut inside rolls around inside.

**4** You should start to hear the eeriest, spookiest sound.

### The Scientific Excuse

A hexagonal nut, of course, has six sides. Each time one of these sides hits the inside of the balloon, as the nut rolls, it creates a little bump or vibration. But of course the nut is rolling very fast, so the pace of the bumps and vibrations gets higher and higher. What we hear as sound is actually air being disturbed and vibrating at a certain rate. The air inside the balloon, bouncing around because of this high-speed bumping, begins to make a high-pitched sound.

# THE *Bubble* CHILD

**EVERYONE, YOUNG AND OLD, HAS BLOWN BUBBLES, SO THERE** doesn't seem much more that can be said about them. But imagine how your most "been there, done that" friend would feel about actually being engulfed in a bubble. This is a great warm weather experiment to perform outdoors. Have a camera ready to record the outcome since there are bound to be doubters when you—or your friend—describe the result. The "secret ingredient" (glycerin) adds color and strength to the bubbles.

*TAKE CARE!* **MAKE SURE THE BUBBLE SOLUTION IS KEPT FROM YOUR FRIEND'S EYES—A PAIR OF GOGGLES MIGHT BE A GOOD PRECAUTION. ALSO BEAR IN MIND THAT THE QUALITY OF BUBBLE VARIES WITH THE TYPE OF WATER BEING USED (SOME WATER HAS NATURALLY OCCURRING MINERALS THAT MAKE IT A BIT HARDER TO DO THE EXPERIMENT). IT'S ALSO BEST TO TRY THIS EXPERIMENT WHEN THE WEATHER IS HUMID.**

## You Will Need

- 2 CUPS DISHWASHING LIQUID
- 3 CUPS TAP WATER
- 1/2 CUP GLYCERIN (SOLD AT MOST PHARMACIES)
- 2-GALLON BUCKET (IDEALLY WITH LID)
- SMALL WADING POOL (MINIMUM 3-FOOT DIAMETER)
- PLASTIC HULA HOOP
- SWIMMING GOGGLES
- SMALL STOOL

# METHOD

**1** Mix the dishwashing liquid, water, and glycerin in the bucket to make the bubble mixture. (This mixture can keep—and even improves over time—but you must cover the bucket.)

**2** Pour the bubble mixture into the pool.

**3** Place the hula hoop in the pool so it's immersed in the solution.

**4** Taking care not to puncture the base of the pool, place the stool inside the hula hoop.

**5** Ask a friend to put on the goggles and stand on the stool—it's always best to choose someone who likes to be thought of as cool, to watch the transformation.

**6** Lift the hula hoop up and over your friend: A giant bubble will engulf them.

## The Scientific Excuse

The dishwashing liquid (soap) is the prime ingredient for any blown bubble. Each soap molecule has two halves—one hydrophilic (attracted to water) and one hydrophobic (repelled by water). The bubble is actually a "sandwich": a layer of water molecules squeezed between two layers of soap molecules. The two enemies of bubbles are water tension and evaporation. The interaction with the soap molecules stretches the water molecules apart, weakening the tension. The other ingredient, glycerin, forms weak hydrogen bonds with the water, slowing or even preventing evaporation.

# Overcoming GRAVITY

YOU CAN CHOOSE THE LEVEL OF IRRESPONSIBILITY FOR THIS experiment, depending on your nerve. You can try it over a table or a sink—or over the head of a very courageous volunteer. No matter which approach you use, it's always fun to see people's shocked expressions if they've never tried this classic experiment demonstrating air pressure.

## You Will Need

- DRINKING GLASS
- WATER
- PLAYING CARD OR POSTCARD
- TOWEL OR TUB (IN CASE OF TROUBLE)

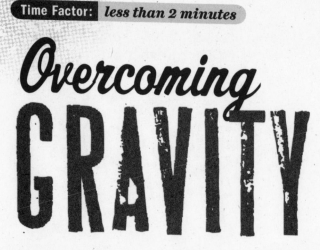

**TAKE CARE!** THE BEST OBJECTS TO COVER THE RIM OF THE GLASS ARE LIGHT BUT FIRM—SO THE PLAYING CARD AND POSTCARD ARE IDEAL. ANYTHING HEAVIER SCORES WELL WITH FIRMNESS BUT MIGHT BE A LITTLE TOO HEAVY FOR THE AIR PRESSURE TO DO ITS TRICK. ANOTHER WORD OF WARNING TO REMEMBER: DON'T KEEP THE GLASS AND CARD OVERTURNED FOR TOO LONG. IF THE CARD BECOMES SOGGY, IT DEFORMS. THAT MAKES IT HARDER FOR THE AIR PRESSURE TO WORK, SO GRAVITY MIGHT SUDDENLY WIN!

# METHOD

**1** Fill the glass three-quarters full with water.

**2** Place the card squarely over the mouth of the glass, making sure that there's no gap.

**3** Pressing the card to the rim, turn the glass over—over your volunteer's head, if you feel brave!

**4** When the glass is upside down, remove your hand from the card.

**5** The card should remain attached to the glass and no water should leak out.

## The Scientific Excuse

The simple explanation to this experiment is that it all depends on air pressure. The water inside the glass certainly presses down on the card, but what's surprising is the strength of the air pressure working in the opposite direction—greater than the force of gravity, in this case.

# The MAGIC NAPKIN

**WELL, THIS AGE-OLD EXPERIMENT COULD JUST AS EASILY** have found its way into a magic book. But at its heart is a basic scientific principle—one of the most basic of those proposed by the great Sir Isaac Newton. No points for figuring out how this one is irresponsible: You'll know in a flash whether it is or it isn't!

## You Will Need

- PAPER NAPKIN
- PLASTIC CUP FULL OF WATER

**TAKE CARE!** YOU CAN DECIDE HOW RISKY OR IRRESPONSIBLE THIS EXPERIMENT IS BY WORKING OUT WHERE TO DO IT. IF THE CUP DOES SPILL, IT MEANS THAT YOU HAVEN'T PULLED QUICKLY ENOUGH OR WITH ENOUGH FORCE. DON'T FORGET THAT THIS BOOK IS ALL ABOUT BEING IRRESPONSIBLE. SOME PEOPLE HAVE GONE THROUGH LIFE ALWAYS GETTING TO STEP 3 BUT NEVER PULLING OFF STEP 4! OTHERS GET IT RIGHT THE FIRST TIME.

# METHOD

**1** Drape the napkin over the edge of a table or kitchen counter.

**2** Put the cup on one corner of the napkin about an inch from the edge of the table.

**3** Securely grasp the overhanging edge of the napkin and quickly pull it out from under the cup.

**4** You should end up with the napkin in your hand and the cup still in place on the table.

## The Scientific Excuse

This experiment demonstrates the principle of inertia, first observed by Sir Isaac Newton as he formulated his famous laws of motion. Inertia describes the tendency of objects to stay at rest—in this case, to stay on the table rather than be tugged away with the napkin.

# CASH OR CHARGE?

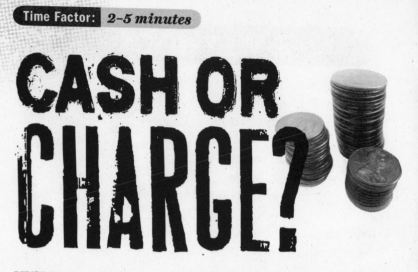

**ISN'T IT SHOCKING THE WAY SOME PEOPLE ARE UNABLE TO** count out change? Here's an experiment that's just as shocking, only this time the shock comes from the coins piling up, not being counted out.

## You Will Need

- 1 CUP LEMON JUICE
- CUP
- PAPER TOWEL(S) CUT INTO ELEVEN 1-INCH SQUARES
- 6 PENNIES
- 6 NICKELS

**TAKE CARE!** THE AMOUNT OF ELECTRICITY PRODUCED HERE IS VERY SLIGHT, SO THERE'S NO RISK INVOLVED. JUST TO MAKE SURE IT ALL WORKS, HOWEVER, MAKE SURE THE PAPER TOWEL SQUARES ARE WET BUT NOT DRIPPING. ALSO, CLEAN COINS WORK BETTER THAN DIRTY ONES.

# METHOD

 **1** Pour the lemon juice into the cup and add the squares of paper towel.

**2** Place the coins in a pile, alternating pennies and nickels, with a lemon-soaked paper square between each coin. (There should be an exposed coin surface at either end of the pile when you finish.)

**3** Moisten the tips of your thumb and index finger and hold the pile of coins between them.

## The Scientific Excuse

The shock you felt was a genuine, if slight, electric shock. Electricity, on one level, can be described as the flow of electrons. In this case, the acidic lemon juice releases a positive charge from the copper-plated pennies and a negative charge from the nickels. That would be the end of it—in other words, the electricity would not "flow"—if the circuit remained incomplete. By holding the pile of coins between your moistened fingers you have completed the circuit, leading to the electric tingle. Normal batteries, such as those in a car or a flashlight, operate on the same principle as this "wet cell."

# The NON-DRIP DOCUMENT

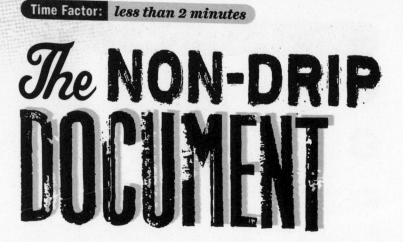

"LESS IS MORE," MODERN ARCHITECT MIES VAN DER ROHE often said, and this simple experiment certainly lives up to the saying. It takes just over a minute to perform, but it gives a great demonstration of some basic science. What's more, the main ingredient—the piece of paper—can become the star attraction. Try making a color photocopy of your brother or sister's homework, or something that belongs to your parents that looks important. This should make the wait in the last stage of this experiment feel like the longest minute your audience has ever endured.

## You Will Need

- SINK OR LARGE BOWL
- WATER
- COPY OF A DOCUMENT (OR AN ORIGINAL IF YOU DON'T MIND CRUMPLING IT UP!)
- CLEAR DRINKING GLASS

**TAKE CARE!** THIS EXPERIMENT IS AN EYE-OPENER EVEN IF YOU DON'T USE A "VALUABLE" PIECE OF PAPER. MAKE SURE—WHATEVER YOU USE—TO SHOVE THE PAPER INTO THE GLASS AS MUCH AS POSSIBLE. YOU DON'T WANT TO RUN THE RISK OF HAVING THE REAL THING FALL OUT BECAUSE YOU DIDN'T SHOVE IT IN HARD ENOUGH.

# METHOD

 **1** Fill the sink or bowl nearly full of water.

 **2** Loosely crumple the paper document.

**3** Shove the crumpled paper into the bottom of the empty glass, tight enough so that it won't fall out when the glass is overturned.

**4** Plunge the glass upside down into the water, deep enough so that the paper appears to be underwater.

**5** Keep the glass in that position for a minute.

 **6** Take the glass out of the water and retrieve the paper; dramatically straighten it and pass it around. It will be dry.

## The Scientific Excuse

The air inside the glass has protected the paper from the water by acting as a barrier. This air is lighter than the water, so it can't flow down through the rim of the glass. At the same time, the water can't flow into the glass because the glass is already full—of air!

# *Introduction to* ALCHEMY

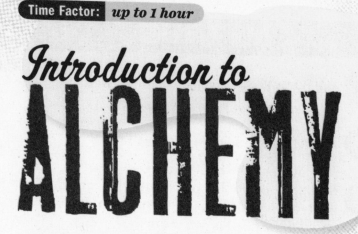

**ALL RIGHT, WE CAN'T PRETEND TO TEACH YOU HOW TO FIND** the Sorcerer's Stone, but this experiment does touch on one of the main aims of the medieval alchemists—changing the nature of metals. Of course, they were looking for a way of turning base metals such as lead into gold, but here you'll have a chance to turn iron into copper. Or at least that's what you'll *seem* to have done.

## You Will Need

- 5/8 CUP VINEGAR
- CERAMIC OR PLASTIC BOWL
- 1 TEASPOON SALT
- 12 PENNIES
  (DULL ONES WORK BEST)
- SPOON
- PAPER TOWEL
- UNGALVANIZED IRON NAIL

# METHOD

**1** Add the vinegar to the bowl, and stir in the salt.

**2** Place the coins in the bowl (adding a little more vinegar if they aren't fully submerged).

**3** Leave the coins in the bowl for 5 minutes.

**4** Retrieve the coins from the bowl using the spoon and let them dry on the paper towel; do *not* dump out the vinegar/salt mixture.

**5** Add the nail to the bowl of liquid and keep it there for 30 minutes. Observe the tiny bubbles forming around it.

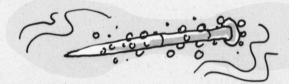

**6** Carefully take the nail out of the bowl and set it on the paper towel to dry. It should appear to be copper!

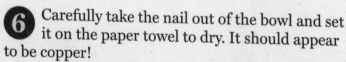

*TAKE CARE!* THIS EXPERIMENT WORKS BEST IF THE CONCENTRATION OF COPPER (FROM THE COINS) IS RELATIVELY HIGH—SO MAKE SURE YOU DON'T OVERDO THE AMOUNT OF VINEGAR YOU USE. DON'T CHOOSE TOO BIG A BOWL, SINCE THE AMOUNT OF LIQUID NEEDED TO COVER THE COINS WOULD WEAKEN THE SOLUTION.

## The Scientific Excuse

In the first stage of the experiment, the vinegar solution "cleaned" some of the copper off the coins. This copper remained in solution (with the vinegar and salt), which in turn had a chemical reaction with the iron on the surface of the nail. As part of this reaction, a chemical exchange left a copper coating on the nail. This type of chemical addition of a metallic layer is called plating; you have created a copper-plated nail. Next stop: gold!

# A GOOD HEAD FOR LIGHTS

**THE PUN IN THIS TITLE MIGHT MAKE YOU GROAN, BUT THE** nifty experiment below has the hallmarks of a classic demonstration: It's quick, easy, and scores high on the "oooh" scale. What's more, there's some really interesting science at its heart. For best results, experiment after dark so the results will appear that much spookier.

## You Will Need

- BALLOON
- VOLUNTEER TO HOLD THE LIGHTBULB
- SECOND VOLUNTEER WITH A GOOD HEAD OF HAIR
- FLUORESCENT LIGHTBULB (15- TO 20-WATT)

# METHOD

 Inflate the balloon and tie it shut.

**2** Have a volunteer hold the lightbulb carefully, with the metal contact pointing outward.

**3** The person holding the balloon should rub it vigorously against his or her head for 10 seconds and then touch it to the metal contact of the fluorescent lightbulb.

**4** The lightbulb should give off a ghostly glow.

## The Scientific Excuse

The gas inside a fluorescent lightbulb becomes "excited" when even a small amount of electricity flows through it. Rubbing the balloon against hair creates static electricity, so when the balloon touches the metal contact, electrons flow into the bulb. This modest electrical charge excites the low-pressure gas inside, which in turn excites the phosphorous coating of the inside the lightbulb. That last stage produces visible white light.

*TAKE CARE!* **MAKE SURE THE VOLUNTEER HANDLING THE FLUORESCENT LIGHTBULB IS CAREFUL AND RESPONSIBLE.**

# LAST WORDS

By now you might find yourself covered in cola and a bit of dripping egg, holding a strangely inflating hand and a drooping chicken leg as you make your way through some thick smoke. Or maybe you'll look a lot neater, with a fan club growing by the minute—kids who want to learn the secrets of your hovering Ping-Pong ball, disappearing milk, and that excellent homemade ice cream.

Either way, you'll know that you've been involved on a journey—into the world of science and its marvelous secrets. If, along the way, you made a little mess, got into some trouble, and maybe wound up looking a bit silly, you're in good scientific company. Don't forget that Isaac Newton probably had a bump on his head for a few days after that famous apple fell. How do we remember him now—as that guy with the funny wig and the ice pack on his head or as the discoverer of gravity?

# AT A GLANCE

Some of the experiments in this book can be done almost in an instant; others take up to several days. The following list groups them in order of time taken, starting with those that can be done most quickly.

## FLASH IN THE PAN (LESS THAN 2 MINUTES)

## 5-MINUTE WONDERS (2–5 MINUTES)

## ON THE HOUR (UP TO 1 HOUR)

## THE 8-HOUR DAY (1–8 HOURS)

## GOING THE DISTANCE (A FULL DAY OR MORE)

# Totally Irresponsible
# NOTES

# Totally Irresponsible NOTES

Totally Irresponsible
# NOTES